"Each story in this book is a balm of hope, resilience, reconciliation, peace, and love, offered by Elena to help a desperate soul feel God's *acompañamiento* while facing adversities in life, … whether as a result of a cruel military regime, loss of a beloved one, terminal illness, extreme poverty, or a natural (or human-made) disaster."

— David A. Vargas, President Emeritus, Division of Overseas Ministries, Christian Church (Disciples of Christ) and former Co-Executive of Global Ministries of the Christian Church (Disciples of Christ) and the United Church of Christ

"*The Earless Man From Chile* takes us on a journey with Elena as she is transformed through the accompaniment of those who touched her life, just as those lives she has touched have been transformed through her years of service as a mission co-worker. She has knitted together 'holy moments' of healing and resilience in ways that allow the reader to feel and touch the lives of our brothers and sisters in Chile. This is ideal reading for Bible study groups or individual spiritual reflection. Thank you, Elena, for allowing us to view the contents of your 'hope chest'."

— Julia Brown Karimu, President, Division of Overseas Ministries, and Co-Executive, Global Ministries of the Christian Church (Disciples of Christ) and the United Church of Christ

"They contend with earthquakes, doubt, suffering, and death. Yet the people in these stories speak of hope. Intricately written, these true tales describe the intimate struggle of embodied faith. The vignettes reveal God as lively and personal, vivid in the touch of a butterfly or the breech of a whale. As they unfold, we see the vision of true shalom coming into vibrant focus."

— Beverly Prestwood-Taylor, Pastor, Athol Congregational Church (UCC), and Executive Director, Brookfield Institute

"During the past twenty years, Elena Huegel has shared her ministry of *acompañamiento,* or of walking alongside, bearing witness to the personal and community stories of the Pentecostal Church of Chile. These are our testimonies of faith. May they bring hope to all who read them!"

— Ulises Munoz, Bishop, Pentecostal Church of Chile

"Elena Huegel's moving vignettes of healing and resilience eloquently portray mutuality in mission with a human face. The collection crosses boundaries of class and North-South interaction and powerfully documents relationships in which we are both host and guest, healer and healed, and fellow travelers on a journey to transformation. Her gift of stories inspires, challenges, and serves as a compass for anyone seeking to follow Jesus in daily life."

— Vernon E. Jantzi, Former Director, Center for Justice and Peacebuilding, Eastern Mennonite University

THE EARLESS MAN FROM CHILE

MISSION STORIES OF HEALING AND RESILIENCE

ELENA HUEGEL

CBP

CHRISTIAN
BOARD OF
PUBLICATION

St. Louis, Missouri

All Scripture quotations are taken from the HOLY BIBLE, NEW INTERNATIONAL VERSION®. NIV®. Copyright © 1973, 1978, 1984 by International Bible Society. Used by permission of Zondervan Publishing House. All rights reserved.

Cover art: Waterfall on the Lircay River at the Shalom Center of the Pentecostal Church of Chile (May 2011). Photo by Elena Huegel.

www.ChalicePress.com

Print: 9780827208476   EPUB: 9780827208483   EPDF: 9780827208490

Library of Congress Cataloging-in-Publication Data

Huegel, Elena.
The earless man from Chile : mission stories of healing and resilience / by Elena Huegel. — First [edition].
    pages cm
Includes bibliographical references and index.
ISBN 978-0-8272-0847-6 (pbk. : alk. paper)
1. Missionary stories. 2. Missions—Chile. 3. Missions—Paraguay. I. Title.

BV2087.H84 2015
266.092—dc23

2015013660

Dedicated to all those who have entrusted me with their stories,
precious gifts I treasure,
and to my family, storytellers one and all!

Contents

LESSONS FROM NATURE

Introduction

Again, the kingdom of heaven is like a merchant looking for fine pearls. When he found one of great value, he went away and sold everything he had and bought it.

MATTHEW 13:45-46[1]

I am on a lifelong treasure hunt, and you have in your hands a journal, of sorts, with a few of the secrets I have discovered. The quest for these hidden riches has taken me up and down the long South American country of Chile, and from there to the United States and back again. "The Earless Man from Chile" and the other stories in this book are pearls uncovered in the depths of the human spirit, inside clam-like souls, formed by the sands of joys and sorrows, learning and doubts, laughter and hope. These stories reveal the mysteries in the healing of relationships and in resilience cultivated by faith. They are pearls threaded together into a necklace that joins the past to the present and draws us toward the future.

As we read, we are transformed by the simplicity of each story and reminded of the common humanity within all of us. We enter for an instant into the eternal present, reliving firsthand the joys and challenges of a personal testimony. It is in that present where a new dream is first envisioned. The story comes to an end, but the endless thread of experience that strings together the exquisite jewelry of relationships remains to be used by both the teller and the listener to craft new treasures. As we sit in the presence of past stories, we are inspired to incorporate the imagination, insight, and fresh understanding we have gained into our own life story.

A life-giving story comes with two inherent and dynamic invitations. One is the invitation to be retold, either by the original teller or by listeners who now become tellers, whereby it changes and grows, taking on the depths and values characteristic of myth. The second is the invitation to the telling of another story, either an old one resonating from the listener's past or a new one conceived

---

[1]All Bible texts taken from the New International Version.

in the moment of the telling and birthed at some later time. Each of us may choose to join in the treasure hunt for these precious story-pearls. However, I must leave you with a word of warning and a piece of advice from one adventurer to another as you read these stories of healing and resilience:

Beware that if you risk stepping into a story,
you may expose yourself to irresistible change.

And:

The best stories connect you to something beyond yourself.
If you keep on the trail of these stories, you will discover
riches heaped upon riches.

RIGHT RELATIONSHIPS

*Pastora Viviana, Hermana Hermita,
and Elena at the San Gerardo Church
of the Pentecostal Church of Chile.*

1

Blest Be the Tie That Binds

And over all these virtues put on love, which binds them
all together in perfect unity.

COLOSSIANS 3:14

During camp at the Shalom Center[1], I loved sleeping in a tent
for two reasons: I could enjoy little moments to myself since no
one else wanted to sleep in a tent, and I felt closer to nature. So, I
was sleeping in a tent at the Shalom Center on February 27, 2010.
It was a warm summer night, and the light of the full moon filtered
through the thin fabric. I awoke a few seconds before 3:34 a.m.,
wondering what had interrupted my sleep. Then I heard rumbling
sounds deep underground. My air mattress bobbed as wave after
wave erupted across the forest floor.

The earthquake lasted for an eternal two minutes and forty-five
seconds. I tried to grab my glasses from the tent pocket and put on
my hiking boots, but the tent poles curled, bending and groaning
in the windless dark. As the falling rocks from the cliff face on the
mountain across from the Shalom Center filled the air with dust and
deafening crashes, I managed to get out of the tent and ring the bell,
calling for the evacuation of the Welcome House. There weren't any
participants at the Shalom Center that weekend, but the staff was
there for a previously scheduled emergency simulation and first aid
training. The plan had been to "practice" what to do in case of an
earthquake. At first, the staff thought that I had somehow conjured
up the power to shake the cabin in order to observe their reactions
and evaluate the training. It took most of them a few moments to
realize that even with my talent for thinking up different challenges
to stimulate experiential education, the severe swaying was beyond

---

[1]The Shalom Center is a peace education, environmental education, and
spiritual development project of the Pentecostal Church of Chile in the Andes
Mountains of the Maule Region of central Chile.

my abilities. The situation gave us the opportunity to laugh together once we were all out in the field and had counted off to make sure everyone was all right.

No one at the Shalom Center was hurt, but in the same minutes that the boulders plummeted from the rock face across from the camp, many homes, churches, workplaces, hospitals, and schools throughout Chile crumbled into ruins. In the coming days and weeks as electricity, water, and communication systems were restored, I learned more about the devastation and marveled at the resilience and solidarity of the Chilean people.

A friend in Massachusetts created a wonderful way to show people where the earthquake occurred and how we responded together as a church to the many needs of the people in Chile.

Starting with about eight inches of four-ply string, imagine that it represents our covenant agreements as the body of Christ. One of the four threads represents the local church—each congregation with its members—committed to praying and sharing resources to build the Kingdom of God. The second thread represents our regions and conferences. The third thread is the North American church and all of its different expressions such as Global Ministries.[2] The fourth thread represents the global church, the body of Christ around the world. When we are all bound together, we are strong. An Ethiopian proverb says: "If threads come together, they can tie the lion."

Now let's imagine that this string is Chile. Like the string, Chile is a very long and thin country, divided into fifteen regions. The Andes Mountains stretch down the length of one side of the country, and on the other side is the Pacific Ocean. If we tie an overhand knot in the middle of the string, it would mark Talca, the city where I live. Imagine the knot looks a bit like a heart.

The earthquake occurred just south of Talca, off the coast between the seventh and eighth regions of Chile. We can represent these two regions by placing two fingers below the knot just tied. The sixth, seventh, and eighth regions of the country were most affected by the earthquake. Place one finger above the knot to represent the sixth region. The three fingers on the string demonstrate how much of the country was torn apart by the earthquake. Of course, other areas were affected, too. About five million people—almost

---

[2]Global Ministries is the organization formed by the United Church of Christ and the Christian Church (Disciples of Christ) as a unified expression of the church in the mission of receiving and sharing with people overseas.

a third of the total population of the country—felt severe tremors.

Now ask someone to tie the string around your wrist. Having someone else tie the knot reminds us that we all depend on and need each other. This new knot that brings the two ends together represents everything that binds us to one another in spite of our differences. We are bound together and committed, through our covenants, to an enduring love for each other. Because we are one body joined together by Christ's love, we pray for, clothe, feed, and shelter those members of our body who are suffering. Many people—both in Chile and around the world—are helping to rebuild homes and lives destroyed by the earthquake.

Finally, see how the heart-shaped knot representing Talca is on one side of the wrist while the knot that joined the two ends together is on the opposite side. People from Chile and the United States live on two different sides of the world, but we are still connected. As you look at the string, remember the meaning of each of the four threads and the two knots. Pray for Chile and for all of our sisters and brothers near and far, bound together in the mission to share God's love.

QUESTIONS

1. What did you know about Chile before you read this story? Have you ever purchased products imported from Chile?
2. What disaster relief activities have you participated in? Make a list of all the activities your church groups could do to help a community recovering from a natural disaster. Which of these things motivate you the most?
3. In what ways do you feel connected to the body of Christ around the world?
4. In what ways do you feel disconnected from the body of Christ around the world? What do you think would help deepen the connection?

2

The Earless Man from Chile

Peace I leave with you; my peace I give you. I do not
give to you as the world gives. Do not let your hearts be
troubled and do not be afraid.

JOHN 14:27

I remember the first time I heard about a country called Chile.
It was in Mexico City, and I was seven or eight years old. In the
afternoons, I played "fútbol," or soccer, with my brothers and the
neighborhood children on a field in front of the buildings that
made up the Union Theological Seminary. We were the children of
students and faculty from all over Latin America, and our games
were spiced by the mix of languages, skin colors, and cultures. One
day, a strange man, leaning heavily on a wooden cane, limped to
the edge of the field and watched us with haunting, absent eyes that
seemed to look right through us to something beyond. I remember
noticing the scars on his face, his trembling hands, his unkempt
look and smell, and the hole in the side of his head where his ear
should have been. He began showing up often, and as children do,
we shied away from him, cautiously whispering among ourselves.

The earless man frightened me, so I asked my father, a
professor at the seminary, about him. My dad pulled me close into
an embrace and tried to explain political violence in a way that a
second grader could understand. "That man is not from Mexico
but from a faraway country called Chile. In that country they have
a leader, a dictator, who hurts anyone who doesn't do what he
wants. This man who watches you play was hurt so badly by the
men who follow the dictator that he had to leave his family, home,
and country. 'Torture' is a horrible way that people with power hurt
other people who think differently. We helped this man escape so
he wouldn't be killed, and now we are trying to aid him until he
can go back home again."

The dictator my father had mentioned was General Augusto Pinochet. On September 11, 1973, when I was seven, General Pinochet had led Chilean troops in a violent coup that overthrew the democratically elected president, issuing in years of repression, torture, and disappearances; some people left to go to work or to the store and were never heard from again. Little did I know then that in January 1996 I would move to the earless man's country. When I arrived in Chile, Pinochet was still the head of the military, though no longer president, and the country was absorbed in a complex healing process. When I ask Chileans 40 years old or older, during those quiet intimate moments in which we allow memories to bubble to the surface, where they were and what they were doing on the morning the presidential palace was bombed, each person brings up a wealth of details as if the events of that day are branded into their minds. Though Chileans have struggled to bring about reconciliation, the collective and individual traumas from the coup and the years of dictatorship are threads woven through every fiber of daily life. Domestic violence and child abuse are prevalent, carefully hidden under a gentlemanly veneer of male dominance. Chilean universities, which were among the best in Latin America before the coup and produced two Nobel Laureates in literature—Gabriela Mistral and Pablo Neruda—are now marked by mediocrity and conformity. Military prowess lurks as a constant undertow in Chile's economic, cultural, and political relationships with its neighbors.

In many ways, the country has not been able to throw off the uniformity of the military; those who did not "wear the uniform" disappeared or had to leave the country. Those who survived learned that to be different in thought or in deed could mean torture or death. Today many people still hide behind the political and social excuses of the military, accepting injustice in the name of peace and tranquility and reacting harshly toward anyone who might try to upset the status quo. Every year on September 11, the country braces for another round of violence bursting forth in a destructive and painful commemoration of justice and truth not yet fully served. Every year, that is, except September 11, 2001.

On that morning, I was at home when the phone rang. "Turn on your television," exclaimed one of my Chilean friends. "Something horrible is happening in the United States." I turned on the set just in time to see the second plane smash into the World Trade Center in New York City. For the first time since 1973, in Chile there were no vandalizing mobs, no bus burnings, and no Molotov cocktails thrown at heavily armed riot police, as the whole country came to a standstill reliving its own September 11 events.

During the next few weeks, I received more phone calls from Chilean friends. "Please tell our sisters and brothers in the United States that we are praying for them." "Please tell United States citizens we are learning to forgive. They can learn to forgive also." I felt surrounded by caring support as I began to unravel my own feelings and reactions to the terrorist attacks and the aftermath of US military interventions that left anyone holding a US passport exposed and vulnerable to globalized phantoms of hate, animosity, and rancor.

Michelle Bachelet, who became the first woman president of Chile in 2006 and was reelected in 2013, was detained in a concentration camp during the Pinochet dictatorship. Her father, a military man on the wrong side of the coup, died in prison in 1974 when he refused to follow the dictator's lead. Today, President Bachelet continues to work toward truth and reconciliation. However, the truth-speaking process has been a slow one. Pinochet, the former dictator, still enjoyed a great deal of popularity until his death in 2006. Perhaps it has been wise to measure carefully the timing of truth committees, torture reports, and military confessions, spreading these out over many years. Some Chileans fear that tipping the scales too quickly might result in more violence, but for those who are victims, justice appears to solidify and then melt away like the fog rising between the Pacific Ocean and Andes Mountains.

Schools opening in March mark the beginning of fall and the new school year in the Southern Hemisphere. In the past couple of years, I have heard Chilean elementary school students stand and read essays on their fears of war. I have listened to groups of teenagers at church praying and interceding for the governments, leaders, people, and children of Iraq, Afghanistan, and the United States. I have sat around many tables in meetings and at meals as members of the Pentecostal Church of Chile[1] try to understand the tangle of current events, feelings, and memories.

Helping individuals and small groups move through the multiple traumas of the dictatorship in Chile has been like putting

---

[1]The Pentecostal Church of Chile has been a Global Ministries partner for many years. It is a nationally born and supported church, a founding member of the Latin American Council of Churches, and an active member of the World Council of Churches.

away the tablecloths, napkins, sheets, and towels that belong in a cedar hope chest after they have been used. Many people attempt to pile all the cloths back into the chest, dirty and crumpled, without examining or restoring them. The chest will not close, and over time, the jumbled cloths will either rot or become useless because of the stains, rips, and wrinkles. However, if we can pull out each memory like a piece of fabric, admiring the weave while mending, washing, ironing, and gently folding, then the remembrances inside the hope chest are available for our use when we need experience and wisdom.

The well-worn memory of the earless man who watched me play as a child is a neatly folded cloth that I have pulled out many times. While reliving my father's embrace, I help others put their hope chests back together. I have learned that the cedar smell of restoration and wholeness can permeate even the most chaotic pile of life's dirty fabric.

QUESTIONS

1. This story tells about the collective trauma of the Chilean society. Can you identify a trauma that your community has suffered?
2. Chileans are slowly coming to terms with this painful period of their history. In what ways has your community begun to heal from its trauma?

3

One Small Step toward Reconciliation

My dear brothers and sisters, take note of this: Everyone
should be quick to listen, slow to speak and slow to
become angry, because human anger does not produce
the righteousness that God desires.

JAMES 1:19-20

There are many points of view in Chile about the United States'
involvement in different countries around the world. I have listened
to Chileans who believe that there are terrorist groups gearing up
to take over the planet; they support any action to eradicate this
threat. I have listened to others who affirm that the United States
is once again playing the role of the global bully. Some say that the
Chilean president should call for a national vote to let the people
decide whether or not to support the United States, while others
fear that terrorism will come again to Chile as it did once before.

During the past years, as a citizen of the United States living
abroad, I have tried to be "quick to listen," and "slow to speak." I
have heard different points of view on the tensions and threats in
the global context. When the United States invaded Iraq, Chile, with
its position on the United Nations Security Council, was caught
between a rock and hard place, or as we would say in Spanish,
"between the sword and the wall." On one hand, many Chileans
felt strongly that the United States should not have gone forward
with a preemptive strike and that the US government should have
submitted to the decisions made in the global forum. Chile does
not wish to pick a fight with countries or groups that might define
themselves as enemies of the United States. Chile does not have
the technology or security systems to protect itself from terrorist
attacks. On the other hand, Chile has had good diplomatic, cultural,

educational, and economic relations with the United States. Chileans know that shunning the United States could be very dangerous, especially if it means economic sanctions.

What happens on the world stage plays itself out unexpectedly in daily life when one lives overseas. I think back to an experience I had with a man from the Curicó church[1] of the Pentecostal Church of Chile. He sought me out after Sunday worship. I had never had the opportunity to talk with this man before, though I often greeted him in church or when we met on the street. I was a little surprised when he came straight up to me, and with a look of anguish on his face, blurted out something about war, the United States, and peace. I didn't understand all of his words, charged as they were with emotion, but his tear-filled eyes and expression spoke louder than the words. My response was something like, "Yes, my brother, pray for peace, and pray that our sisters and brothers in the United States might be given wisdom and strength." He was so choked up that he was not able to say another word but just nodded and shook my hand before walking away.

A couple of weeks later, he stopped me outside before the Sunday afternoon worship service. I had been translating for a delegation from the Massachusetts Conference of the United Church of Christ during the annual meeting of the Pentecostal Church of Chile and had been very visible during the week. As the delegates walked on ahead, this brother gently touched my arm and asked if he could have a word with me. "I come to beg your forgiveness, my sister," he said. "When I came to you a few weeks ago, I had intended to vent all of my anger and pain on you. When you told me to pray for our brothers and sisters in the United States and to pray for peace, that was not the response I expected from you. I was not able then to say what I was thinking or feeling. I had never thought that I could pray for the people of the United States and its government. I must tell you that during all the years that you have been here in our church and in our country, I have not been able to accept anything you have done or said. I have felt deep rejection of you, your country, and all that the United States represents. Please, please forgive me."

---

[1]The Curicó church of the Pentecostal Church of Chile is the "mother" church from which the denomination began to spread to every region in the country. It is also the "cathedral," and the local pastor serves as bishop to the denomination, which has Methodist roots.

I kept silent and let him continue talking between tears and sobs. "I was a socialist and a prisoner of war in my own country. I know what it is like to be in a concentration camp, and the torture I suffered, no human being should ever have to live through."

At that moment, I began to understand. This man, my brother in Christ, had lived in the flesh the results of the coup in Chile and the dictatorship. I realized that he also knew of the US government's involvement in Chile in support of the coup and the military regime's horrendous violation of human rights. Most Americans do not remember that on the 11th of September 1973, the United States naval forces were stationed off the coast of Valparaiso, Chile, to provide assistance in case the coup was not successful. The CIA had been involved in a propaganda campaign to discredit the democratically elected socialist president and had helped pave the way for the military to take over the country. Most Americans do not realize that Chileans feel inexorably tied to the United States because of this past history in the midst of the economic, cultural, and political results of modern globalization. Most Americans do not know that throughout Chile, people set aside their differences on the 11th of September 2001 and showed their compassion, empathy, and solidarity by participating in prayer vigils for the United States. However, I do know these things. I struggle constantly to balance my deep appreciation of the values, opportunities, and privileges I have received as a citizen of the United States with the calling I feel as a follower of Christ to be present with and connected to his body around the world.

My brother from the Curicó church searched to find words to finish his confession. "Please forgive me for not accepting you." I reached out and hugged this older man and then whispered to him, "It is I who must ask for your forgiveness." He stared at me with a puzzled look. I continued. "Please forgive my country for its part in your suffering and pain. Please forgive my people for what they did to yours." I could see his defenses coming off like a knight removing his armor. He clung to me for a few moments, and we wept. Finally he looked at me straight in the eyes as if to catch any evasion on my part when he stated, "You know, then. You know your people taught my people how to torture." I nodded, looking down in shame. Then he continued, his voice turning soft with compassion, "I would like to tell you more. Can we have tea together someday?"

In the Chilean culture, an invitation to tea is an invitation to relationship, to deeper understanding, to the space of truth around the breaking of bread. With this invitation to share at his table in his home, I began to pray for the grace to listen with compassionate ears and a humble heart.

This brother from the Curicó church and I were never able to share afternoon tea. Shortly after our conversation, he became very ill and then died suddenly. His untimely death was traced to severe health problems caused by the torture he had suffered. I cherish the memory of his confession and forgiveness, because it reminds me, in the midst of the confusion, fear, hate, and conflicting information presented in the news, that together we took one small step through truth, justice, and mercy toward reconciliation.

QUESTIONS

1. What do you most appreciate about this story?
2. Is there any part of this story that is difficult for you to listen to?
3. What questions do you think you would have asked if you had the opportunity to share a cup of tea with the brother from the Curicó church?

4

"Reencuentros"

I will listen to what God the LORD says;
    he promises peace to his people, his faithful servants—
    but let them not turn to folly.
Surely his salvation is near those who fear him,
    that his glory may dwell in our land.

Love and faithfulness meet together;
    righteousness and peace kiss each other.
Faithfulness springs forth from the earth,
    and righteousness looks down from heaven.
The LORD will indeed give what is good,
    and our land will yield its harvest.
Righteousness goes before him
    and prepares the way for his steps.

                        PSALM 85:8-13

I recently heard Michelle Bachelet[1], a former president of Chile, try to explain in English the not easily translatable Spanish word "reencuentro." Her dilemma was particularly interesting to me because the Shalom Center's motto is "un lugar de reencuentro," which we have loosely translated as "a gathering place." "Reencuentro" could be translated as "reencounter," but the English word doesn't carry the rich connotation of coming back together after a long absence, of walking forward in a spiral that leads back to memories, places, experiences, and people but from a different point of view, or of gathering pieces of the old and weaving them into new relationships. For the Shalom Center of the Pentecostal Church of Chile, "reencuentro" speaks of a holistic reconciliation with God, self, others, and creation.

---

[1]Michelle Bachelet has recently been reelected president of Chile. In Chile, former presidents may run for reelection in non-consecutive terms.

Not long ago, I was invited to travel from Chile to Mexico by the Mesa Conjunta[2] to participate as a facilitator at the Latin American Youth Leadership Conference. The journey for me was one of "reencuentros."

I grew up in Mexico, principally in Mexico City and Guadalajara, and by the age of seventeen when I left to go to college in the United States, I had visited 29 of Mexico's 31 states. Since my parents and my paternal grandparents were missionaries with the Christian Church (Disciples of Christ) in Mexico, I returned home there whenever I had the chance. Missionary families, just like families in the United States, face the normal stresses of daily life: sick children, rebellious adolescents, moves, educational decisions, worship options, conflicts with coworkers. However, these normal challenges, when compounded by the juggling of multiple cultures, languages, and worldviews, can create disorienting storms of throbbing bewilderment. At the same time that I moved away from home in Mexico to start my first year of college in Texas, my parents entered a painful and confusing process of separation.

A few years after college, I moved back to Mexico and lived with my father in the city of San Luis Potosí where he helped to establish the Center for Theological Studies of the Christian Church (Disciples of Christ) in Mexico. I saw my mother occasionally when visiting Mexico City. These were difficult times for my family. I remember endless discussions about "God's will," with my mother convinced we were being called as a family to continue ministering in Mexico City, a teeming metropolis with the pressing needs of one of the largest populations in the world. Meanwhile, my father felt fulfilled and happy with the new seminary project in San Luis Potosí, and each of my brothers and I were excited about pursuing our own dreams and future professions. None of us intended to move back to Mexico City, and by the end of the year, I took the leap toward independence and left for the Jack Norment Camp in Paraguay, where I facilitated the environmental education program.

As I left my family behind and ventured out on my own to a country I had never visited before and to a people I had never met, I prayed, making a deal with God. I promised I would serve the Lord faithfully with all of my heart, mind, and body, but I depended on God fulfilling what I perceived as God's part of the bargain: that

---

[2]Joint Board for Mission Development in Mexico representing the Christian Churches (Disciples of Christ) in Mexico and the Congregational Churches in Mexico.

my family would be gently protected and cared for in the midst of the unresolved conflicts between my parents.

A few short weeks after I left for Paraguay, the Disciples of Christ churches in Mexico exploded in an agonizing conflict that not only split the denomination, but divided many local congregations and families. The seminary my father had worked so hard to found was closed, and his former students left, some to continue their ministerial studies and others to seek out other ways to serve God. For my mother, this was another sign that God wanted us to return to Mexico City, but my father's missionary appointment was redefined; this time he was assigned to serve with the Christian Congregational Churches[3] in Mexico, based in Guadalajara.

While my parents continued to struggle with their relationship and their differing calls to ministry, I felt that God was fulfilling "the desires of my heart" as expressed in Psalm 37:4, one of my favorite Bible texts: "Take delight in the LORD, and he will give you the desires of your heart." I had asked God to take me to a Christian camp in South America where I could teach environmental education to people of all ages and exercise my creativity to the fullest. At the Jack Norment camp, I discovered and honed the gifts of teaching through storytelling, theater, dialogue, and empathetic listening that God had bestowed on me to strengthen and deepen my ministry as a missionary.

I also discovered that many of the challenges faced by the church in Mexico were similar to the ones in the Christian Church, Disciples of Christ, in Paraguay, and that churches and denominations in other countries suffer splits much like families do. Some church conflicts, however, are exacerbated by longtime sociopolitical patterns set by colonialism, the ingrained inheritance of oppression, economic models that maintain a broad distance between the rich and the poor, the engulfing and relentless march of globalization, and in Latin America, the historic dominance of the Catholic Church.

The Reverend David Vargas, then the Executive Secretary for the Latin America and the Caribbean office of Global Ministries and later Co-Executive of this same organization, visited Paraguay while I was there. He took time out from his busy schedule to sit down with me for a long talk. Pastor David knew my family situation and the scenario in the Disciples church in Mexico and Paraguay all too well. He had strained to hold together the pieces

---

[3]Historically connected to the United Church of Christ

of the Christian Church, Disciples of Christ in Mexico until the splintered shards were forced out of his hands. Yet he spoke to me that day at the Jack Norment Camp in Paraguay with what, by the grace of God, would turn out to be a prophetic voice, similar in my mind to those wild Old Testament dreams announcing a future time of peace and reconciliation. He told me that he had asked God to grant him the privilege of witnessing two miracles before he retired from Global Ministries: one was the healing of my parents' relationship, and the other, the building of a bridge across the rift in the Disciples church in Mexico. It seemed as impossible to me as the Isaiah announcements of the coming hope and joy of the Messiah must have seemed to the downtrodden people of Israel. I wanted to believe in reconciliation, but the evidence embedded in the bitter words and hurtful memories both in the church and in my family made me doubt.

To return to the Christian Church, Disciples of Christ, in Mexico after so many years was, as I said before, one of "reencuentros," of coming full circle back to the beginnings of my missionary family. I visited the church in San Luis Potosí where my grandparents initiated their missionary service in Mexico. I remembered the stories about my aunt who died as an infant and was buried in the cemetery of the city and how that experience stretched my grandparents' faith to the limit. I stood outside the colonial building in Aguascalientes where the missionaries used to live and where my father was born. I visited the little village of Los Nogales, Zacatecas, where my father had his first pastorate, and I took pictures of the weather-beaten adobe house where he proposed to my mother. I preached in the Disciples church in Guadalajara, the church that accompanied both of my parents even as their lives took separate paths. I traveled to Texas, reliving the many border crossings of my childhood, some traumatic and some verging on bizarre. I remembered, for example, the time the US border patrol took our old car apart removing seats, tires, and every scrap of personal effects and luggage searching for drugs. They then left my parents with four small children all under ten years of age to try to figure out how to put everything back together again.

After all of the traveling, I arrived at the youth retreat where I had been invited to help with the facilitation. It was at the Center for Theological Studies in San Luis Potosí, the seminary my father had established before the denominational split. My grandfather's portrait hung on the wall in the library. After I assigned a group-building task, I sat back to observe the youth from three different denominations…some of whose parents were my friends when we were teenagers and others whose grandparents worked with my parents. The youth from both Disciples denominations and the Congregational Church of Mexico worked together to organize this "reencuentro," making a strong and clear statement to the leadership of all three churches about their desire to face the past, learn from both the gifts and the problems, and dream of a future where they could assume their responsibility to live out the well-known motto "in essentials unity, in non-essentials liberty, and in all things love." Pastor Vargas was there too, on hand to add his bricks of wisdom and experience to the building of the long-awaited bridge. Pastor Vargas once told me that he could keep believing in the miracle of forgiveness offered in Christ because he had seen it in my parents. My parents are now retired and living together, enjoying each other's company, spicing their disagreements with laughter and humility, praying faithfully for and communicating with their children living in four different countries, and pursuing their individual interests and needs. God answered both of those prophetic requests Pastor Vargas had made in Paraguay ten years earlier. After many years of waiting and before his retirement from Global Ministries, reconciliation was coming, bit by bit, to the church in Mexico just as it had come to my parents' marriage.

With Pastor Vargas's example, may we be encouraged to speak out prophetically in the midst of violence, disunity, and brokenness, declaring by faith the reconciliation that perhaps no one else can believe to be possible. May God grant each of us the privilege of a journey of "reencuentros" as described in Psalm 85:10: *Love and faithfulness meet together; righteousness and peace kiss each other.*

QUESTIONS

1. Have you ever experienced a "reencuentro," a coming back together in reconciliation and healing? What was it like?
2. What are the essential elements of a reconciliation process for a church, a community, or a family?
3. Do you pray for any "reencuentros" for your family, community, or church?

5

A Gift to Share

Bear with each other and forgive one another if any of
you has a grievance against someone. Forgive as the
Lord forgave you.

COLOSSIANS 3:13

We met soon after I knew I would be living and serving as a
missionary with Global Ministries in the Pentecostal Church of
Chile. He and his family hosted me, and his two teenage daughters
and I quickly became friends. His comment when we said good-
bye after that first visit was, "I can see that God will use you to
bring many blessings to our church." Those words inspired and
comforted me as I set out to a new life in a country then unknown
to me.

What went wrong? Perhaps I will never know for sure,
but somewhere in the first few years of service in Chile, our
relationship cracked and the rift between us grew. I began to dread
the moments when our paths would cross in meetings or church
gatherings. Rumors wound their way back to me of his ill-spoken
words whenever my name was mentioned in the churches where
I was ministering. It all came to a head at a national assembly of
the Pentecostal Church of Chile. I suppose that most missionaries
and pastors have had similar experiences, and perhaps not once
but many times; it was the first time for me. I found myself
unprepared to face the full-fledged attack of an antagonist. He
spoke passionately to the assembly, finding fault in the programs
and projects to which I was assigned, and afterward he continued
to openly criticize my work.

What could I do? I prayed, and I sought the wisdom of national
leaders and spiritual guides. I analyzed my work, going over every
decision I made as if under a microscope, even to the point of
doubting God's leading. I talked to my supervisors, and I listened
to the frustration of my coworkers. I kept going, participating in

activities and meetings even when it almost became too painful to bear. When one of the ministries I worked with was asked to lead a regional workshop for teachers at my antagonist's church, the other members of the committee wanted to request a change in location. "No," I said, "there must be some reason God has opened the doors for us to be at that particular church. Let's go!" I went trembling with fear, but we had a wonderful time and were affectionately received by the members of the church. He, as the pastor of that congregation, made all of the arrangements and greeted us when we arrived but then left us to continue the workshop on our own.

I didn't go out of my way to meet him, but I didn't avoid him even though my heart raced and my palms sweated every time I had to greet him with the customary handshake and kiss on the cheek. To refuse to do so in the Chilean culture would have been like declaring war against him.

My colleagues accused me of being too hard on my friends and too easy on my enemies, and some went as far as to recommend that I counterattack or at least seek ways to defend myself when he once again attempted to humiliate me in some gathering. I knew that to maintain my dignity, I had to also uphold the dignity of my adversary. If I retaliated, I would damage my own dignity and violate his as well, so I waited and I prayed. I asked my prayer partners to intercede, asking God to prepare me as well as my adversary for any opportunity that might open to step across the rift.

Then the Shalom Center Committee organized a conflict transformation workshop, and he, as an influential pastor, was appointed by the bishop to represent the directorate of the national church. I helped lead the workshop, and just the thought of his presence there made my stomach do flip-flops. I prayed, pleading that the Holy Spirit might intercede and the workshop be the opportunity for the seed of peace to be planted between us.

During the workshop, he was an attentive and insightful student. After an assignment where each person was to map their conflict history, he sought me out. He explained his map to me, telling of childhood abuse, leaving school before graduation to work, menial labor, and struggles just to eat and survive. I listened. I thanked him for sharing his story with me. His eyes filled with tears as he turned away from me and said, "Now maybe you will understand." At that moment, the fear that had been a cold stone in my stomach melted into compassion.

Then it was time again for the annual meeting of pastors. Ever since that first open battle five years ago, I had dreaded the assembly. I always asked, "What is going to happen to me this time? What plans does he have to hurt me?"

As I stood in a corner after the final worship service waiting for a young woman who had sung in the choir, I saw him striding toward me. I checked my stomach. The compassion was still there calming my fear. He hugged me and began to weep. He asked me to forgive him. He said he was sorry for all of the ways that he had hurt me, criticized my ministry, and degraded those with whom I serve.

I had already forgiven him when he made himself vulnerable to me and shared his story with me during the workshop, but now I had the privilege of saying the words, "I forgive you." I accepted his hug by daring to trust as he accepted mine with a humility I had never seen in him before. From that day on, we have shared the gift of forgiveness.

QUESTIONS

1. Have you ever experienced the challenge of an antagonist in your family, work, or church?
2. Did you have the opportunity for reconciliation with that person?
3. How do you deal with situations where you feel that your dignity is attacked? How can we uphold the dignity of our adversaries in the midst of a conflict?

6

Compassion Ripples

With great power the apostles continued to testify to the resurrection of the Lord Jesus. And God's grace was so powerfully at work in them all that there were no needy persons among them. For from time to time those who owned land or houses sold them, brought the money from the sales and put it at the apostles' feet, and it was distributed to anyone who had need.

ACTS 4:33-35

An elderly widow is cutting coupons and saving every extra penny for a special offering to be held at church. With her husband and her children gone, she has to make every cent count. She is not a sweet little old church lady, but one of those crotchety complainers who doesn't want any changes to come to her congregation or her community. Yet, she is saving the pennies from each coupon she uses at the store for the offering she will give to help build a Blessing Cabin[1] in Chile on the other side of the world.

He traveled overseas with a church group when he was fifteen years old. He sang, worked, and made friends with teenagers who spoke a different language but worshipped the same God. When he heard the news, he knew he had to do something to help. So, he designed and made T-shirts imprinted with a drawing of a small house. Now he is selling the T-shirts to raise money to help build Blessing Cabins for the people he learned to love in Chile, that faraway country on the other side of the world.

Eighty men and a few women gather at dusk after a long workday. They are building Blessing Cabins to shelter as many brothers and sisters as they can before the winter rains begin. They

---

[1]The Blessing Cabins were a part of the "Lift Up Hope" project of the Pentecostal Church of Chile for restoration and reconstruction after the February 27, 2010 earthquake and tsunami.

work until late, night after night, week after week, volunteering after their regular jobs, continuing all day on Saturdays, and stopping only for church services on Sunday afternoons. Though small, the Blessing Cabins now taking form in the skilled hands of these volunteer carpenters and master builders are not only dry and warm, but pretty and worthy of the families who will inhabit them. The resources for the building materials have come from offerings given in churches on the other side of the world.

Richard has been watching closely over the small congregation in his care for several weeks, scrambling to scrounge up food, water, clothing, and tents. After the first devastating dawn, the full moon filled him with hope even as the sun disappeared each day and still there was no electricity or running water. His concern grew as the moon began to wane and the days shortened, signaling the rapid passing of the summer and the arrival of the first winter rains. The first three Blessing Cabins arrived just in time, small but sturdy defenses against the bitter winds, put together by the efforts of sisters and brothers nearby and on the other side of the world.

Valentina went to bed Friday night thinking about having fun on the last weekend before her senior year in high school. She awoke at 3:34 in the morning to a thundering roar in the pitch-blackness. Everything in her room began to fall, crashing to the floor as the earth itself convulsed. Her mother screamed. The roof caved in. Then, after two minutes and forty-five seconds of terror came the silence. In the first trembling light of dawn, neighbors pulled Valentina unhurt from the rubble. Her father and pregnant mother died when they ran back inside the house in an attempt to rescue her. When Valentina lost her parents and her home, her church family embraced her with tender care, and within two weeks, Richard and the volunteer builders had her settled, with her sister, into a new Blessing Cabin. Valentina started back to school as soon as it reopened with a new determination to graduate and to be the first in her family to finish high school. She dares to dream again of college and a career. Valentina, whose name is derived from the word for "courage" in Spanish, experienced the ripples of compassion spreading throughout Chile and arriving from around the world after the February 27, 2010 earthquake.

Courageous compassion is throwing a stone in a pool of water, watching it disappear, and believing that the ripples will spread out beyond the scope of the initial action. When we dare to do something for others, whether it be as simple as snipping coupons or selling T-shirts or as sacrificial as caring for a community during a national emergency or running back inside a falling house to save a daughter's life, we create invisible wavelets encircling people thousands of miles away. Either as individuals or as communities of faith, whether we are able to witness the effects or not, we are called to send compassion ripples around the world by giving of ourselves to those in need.

QUESTIONS

1. In what ways are you and your community part of the "compassion ripples" that reach around the world?
2. In what ways have you or your community been a recipient of those "compassion ripples"?
3. How does doing something for others change our lives, too?

7

The House That Love Built

Therefore everyone who hears these words of mine and
puts them into practice is like a wise man who built his
house on the rock. The rain came down, the streams
rose, and the winds blew and beat against that house;
yet it did not fall, because it had its foundation on the
rock.

MATTHEW 7:24-25

I will never forget your beautiful smile. We met a year after
the devastating earthquake in Chile. Your two little boys, shirtless
and shoeless in the summer heat, were playing on a rope swing
underneath bunches of purple grapes hanging from the vine that
crept along the porch beams of your home. You brought me into
your simple wood frame house, your face shining with pride
and tears of joy. You explained how your adobe house had come
crashing down on the night of the earthquake as you, your children,
and your husband clambered out onto the porch. The porch, with
its tangled old grapevine, is all that remains of your former adobe
home.

You told me that you wouldn't give up this clean, dignified,
and hospitable little house even if someone offered you a palace.
"This home is blessed," you said, "because it was built by love."
Love of your sisters and brothers thousands of miles away in the
United States who heard about the earthquake, prayed about what
to do, and organized to send an offering for the Blessing Cabins in
Chile through Global Ministries. Love of your brothers and sisters
from the national Pentecostal Church of Chile who worked with
you to build the new house. Love of the brothers and sisters from
your local congregation who provided the clothing, furniture, and
kitchen utensils needed to replace what was buried in the rubble.

The gratitude in your heart wells up in your smile. This kind of gratitude is contagious, and I can't help but look into your eyes and affirm, rejoicing, "Yes, this is the house that Love built."

QUESTIONS

1. What makes it possible for us to rejoice with gratitude even in the face of difficult circumstances?
2. Think about what you are grateful for and look for an opportunity to share your gratitude with someone else.

8

A Boy's Gift

Here is a boy with five small barley loaves and two
small fish, but how far will they go among so many?
JOHN 6:9

"Tía Elena," he whispered, and I turned around when I heard
his six-year-old voice speaking the polite and respectful title,
"aunt," which the children in the Pentecostal Church of Chile use for
adults even if they are not blood relatives. I knelt down, looking first
into his eyes before noticing his unwiped nose, dirty face, tousled
hair, and grubby clothes. These children from Dichato, the fishing
village north of Concepción, always came to church clean before the
earthquake and tsunami, but now there hadn't been water for many
weeks, and the emergency tents were not enough protection against
the chill of the fall weather. Lack of water, sickness, and personal
hygiene are just a few of the challenges for these children who
escaped the five monstrous waves that crashed over their village.

"Tía," the boy repeated, "these are for you." He opened his
fist to place three warm, semi-melted caramel candies in my hand.
I thanked him as I unwrapped one and placed it in my mouth,
savoring the taste of generosity, the sweetness of a heart willing to
share not from the lack of material things but from the abundance
of the spirit.

When I fear that my gifts of hugs, listening ears, and walking
alongside are minuscule contributions among so many people and
their great needs, I remember that Jesus will bless my generosity
and multiply it beyond the limits of my imagination. Like the
loaves and fishes in Jesus' times, those three squishy candies will
multiply in the hearts of you who have read about the boy's gift.
Through you this story will grow to bless the hungry in body and
spirit thousands of miles away from Dichato, and one little boy's
gift will continue to feed the hearts of many.

QUESTIONS

1. How has your life been blessed by a simple gift?
2. Prepare a simple gift for someone you know who needs to be reminded of God's love.

9

On the Side of the Highway

People were also bringing babies to Jesus for him to place his hands on them. When the disciples saw this, they rebuked them. But Jesus called the children to him and said, "Let the little children come to me, and do not hinder them, for the kingdom of God belongs to such as these. Truly I tell you, anyone who will not receive the kingdom of God like a little child will never enter it."

LUKE 18:15-17

A small hooded figure holding an umbrella, scanty shelter against the pelting rain, stood on the side of a rarely traveled highway in southern Chile. As I sped by, windshield wipers swishing, it took me a mile or so to react. Had the child been selling something wrapped in a towel? Sometimes my curiosity gets the best of me. I turned the car around and went back.

His hands barely reached the window frame as he pulled himself onto the running board to peer into the pickup truck.

"What are you selling?" I asked.

Silence.

"Tortilla de rescoldo?" (Chilean bread cooked in hot ashes.) I tried a different question.

A nod.

"How much are they?"

"Mil pesos." (About two US dollars.) The boy finally whispered an answer, his curious eyes sweeping over me as the rain came in through the open window and dripped down his nose. He clenched the umbrella in one hand and the package in the other as another gust of wind shook the truck.

"How many do you have left to sell?"

"Dos." His lisp revealed just how young he was as he held up two fingers.

"Does your mother make the tortillas?"

30

"Yes." Then warming up a bit as I pulled out the money, he added, "and I sell them for her after school."

His parting gift was a big smile as he counted the money carefully, waved good-bye, and disappeared down a muddy path.

I sat for a moment before putting the truck into gear, thinking about the working children I have met throughout Latin America. I remembered Miguel who watched the bishop's car one night outside the supermarket in Curicó. I sat down on the curb with him and asked him why at ten o'clock he wasn't at home. "I don't dare to go home if I haven't earned $2,000 pesos (about four dollars) first," he answered. "My uncle would beat me if I did."

I remembered the older sister, about ten years old, selling small card calendars from table to table in the food court of a mall in Santiago while hiding from the security guards. "Have you had dinner?" I asked. She shook her head. "I don't need a calendar, but what would you like to eat?" She pointed to the pizza counter. I bought her a pizza and a glass of juice. She clutched it and nearly ran, glancing at me over her shoulder, to an unobtrusive table in the corner where she was joined by her younger brother. There she carefully divided up the pizza and shared the glass of juice, keeping a wary eye on her surroundings.

I remembered the boy selling chewing gum always on the same corner every week as I drove by. I felt like I watched him grow up, any conversation limited by his physical impairment and the timing of the red light.

And I thought wearily about the internal debate I have each time I encounter another child working to help support his or her family, situations so different from my carefree childhood of school and playtime. If I buy from a child selling something on the street, am I exacerbating a cruel cycle of child labor? But how can I pass a child by—not all the children of Chile or the world, but this particular individual standing in the rain, watching a car, or selling calendars and chewing gum? I shift the pickup truck into gear, look back through the rain to make sure no cars are coming, and pull ~~back~~ out onto the pavement. It is getting dark on a solitary highway in southern Chile, and I am just one person, touching one life at a time, as best I can.

QUESTIONS

1. How do you feel about working children? Are there any reasons that justify a child having to work?

2. What do you think are the different points of view in regards to child labor? How do economics and culture influence this debate?
3. In each of the above situations, the author responded in different ways. Which do you think was the most appropriate?
4. Why do you think a missionary should be concerned about "exacerbating a cruel cycle of child labor" in the country where she is serving?

10

Kidnapped

But the wisdom that comes from heaven is first of
all pure; then peace-loving, considerate, submissive,
full of mercy and good fruit, impartial and sincere.
Peacemakers who sow in peace reap a harvest of
righteousness.

JAMES 3:17-18

There is a cedar chest in my father's house. It was my grandmother's "hope chest." Throughout her youth she collected and kept those special items that used to be considered essential upon marriage and the establishment of a new home: linen tablecloths, embroidered napkins, handmade quilts and afghans, fine sheets and towels. In my mind, I too have a hope chest. It is full of the stories I have been given over the years, precious treasures that bear witness to the steadfast love of God and the faithfulness of God's children. After the earthquake in Chile, we had several events at the Shalom Center where I heard many unique stories. At the Roots in the Ruins: Hope in Trauma courses and the Challenge for Resilience retreats,[1] the participants were able to take a step back from the daily problems arising from the catastrophe. They shared their testimonies about God's miraculous provision of courage and persistence in the face of overwhelming circumstances, as well as the personal cost of leadership and compassion. In many cases, the stories about the current situation had roots in past experiences that occurred long before this disaster. We all agreed that the trauma of the earthquake and tsunami provided an unprecedented

---

[1]Roots in the Ruins: Hope in Trauma is a spiritual accompaniment program to nourish hope in the midst of trauma and has been developed by the Shalom Center in collaboration with the Brookfield Institute of Massachusetts. The Challenge for Resilience retreats were held at the Shalom Center for emergency personnel and long-term care providers who served in the earthquake.

opportunity to heal from wounds buried in our pasts. To seek wholeness in the present and build a new future, we had to dare to work through the past.

I asked Lorena, a preschool teacher and Roots in the Ruins participant who also helped lead a Challenge for Resilience retreat, to write her story of healing and reconciliation:

> Many years ago in a poor neighborhood in Curicó, a woman named Paula kidnapped a four-year-old child with the intention of selling her. She walked with the child from Curicó to Molina, about ten miles, without giving her any food or telling her where they were going. That little girl was very frightened, and even though she was young, she feared she would never see her family again. She had reached out her hand and trusted the wrong person, and now she had no choice but to follow and keep walking.
>
> But not all was lost. Her six-year-old brother was praying, asking God for help to find his little sister. The prayer was heard and the miracle came. The child was found and returned to her family.
>
> The kidnapping, however, marked her life. Her personality changed from bubbly and friendly to timid and reserved. She had many fears and anxieties, but at the same time, her faith and trust in Jesus was growing. She never forgot the experience, but learned to be happy in spite of it.
>
> "I am that little girl," Lorena explained as we sat together in the healing circle. Then she continued with her story.
>
> Life has strange twists and turns. A few weeks ago, I participated in the graduation of my beautiful preschool students. Many people were in attendance: parents and grandparents, uncles and aunts, older and younger brothers and sisters. Two large groups of children were graduating, so I did not know most of the people mingling around the school. Moments after the ceremony, I spotted a little girl crying by herself. I could tell she was afraid and apprehensive, but no one seemed to notice her in the crowded courtyard. I drew close, held out my hand to her, and knelt to look into her eyes without saying a word, my heart filling with tenderness. She did not doubt, but took my hand. I stayed at her side, first whispering words of consolation and then introducing myself and inviting her

to tell me her name and age. She was only four years old, a sweet little brunette with laugh crinkles around her eyes.

I didn't expect it when she threw her arms around my neck and kissed my cheek. At that same moment, with the child's trust firmly and freely given to me, I felt a light tap on my shoulder. I looked up to see a woman staring at me, her startled look exposing her shock and alarm. We recognized each other. It was her. Yes, precisely, her. This child lost in the crowd and whom I comforted until her mother found us, was none other than the daughter of the woman who had kidnapped me long ago! The story rewound playing through my mind. Now I was a twenty-three-year-old woman extending her hand to a little four-year-old, exactly the way that so long ago this woman of the same age had held out her hand to me. The difference was that I gave back, without hesitation, the well-being and safety which I had been denied as a child.

I do not doubt that it was God who gave me the opportunity to live, in the space of one heaven-touching-earth instant, that place of healing where truth, justice, mercy, and peace come together and embrace.

QUESTIONS

1. Read Psalm 85:8-15 and compare it to James 3:17-18. What do these texts say about the relationship between justice and peace?
2. Even though Lorena did not receive justice through the legal system, she feels that in her case justice has been served. Why do you think that she feels this way?
3. Some people feel that justice is served creatively when they are able to do something so that others might not suffer the same injustice or trauma. Do you know of any organizations that are expressions of creative justice?

11

A Time to Talk and a
Time to Listen

There is a time for…listening and speaking.

ECCLESIASTES 3:7B

"To take a step back doesn't mean to give up." At the beginning of the "Mediacción[1]" workshops for youth, we make a commitment to create a safe space through a community covenant. Each of us speaks about what we need in order to test new abilities and behaviors without teasing, gossip, nicknames, or blaming and with the possibility of growing from our mistakes. We are, however, human; we break our covenants. The safe space is fragile.

The covenant invites us to live creatively together while considering our personal needs, age differences, spiritual experiences, opinions, personalities, political views, or socioeconomic positions. A covenant doesn't consist of a set of rules, but of agreements or promises that outline the way we will treat each other, how we will live together as a group, and how we will care for the environment around us. While we live in a world of rules and regulations dictated by the authorities, the Bible speaks of covenants by which we commit to right relationships. When a law or a rule is broken, there is punishment and compensation. When a covenant is broken, the relationships in the community are damaged, but the covenant itself offers the way toward understanding, forgiveness, reconciliation, and a renewed commitment. If we all commit to fulfilling our covenant, even when we have hurt each other, then

---

[1]Conflict transformation and mediation program for teenagers created by the Shalom Center. It is called "Mediacción" as a word play that combines the words for mediation and action in Spanish.

we create a safe space that enfolds every individual as well as the community as a whole.

In the first hour of our camp, we come back to the covenant we created months ago when we began to meet together, and we revisit our needs, recognizing our successes and our failures. After submitting the schedule to the community for review, one of our agreements is to respect the need, especially of the adults, to get enough rest. The first night at the Shalom Center everyone is excited to be in a new space far from parents, teachers, pastors, and norms that rule our regular lives. The emotion of the moment overflows, pushing the limits of the agreements we have made, and our safe space falls apart. At bedtime, conversations among the youth become louder and louder and the laughter, along with shoes and pillows, bounce against the wood frame cabin. No one sleeps until the wee hours of the morning when the adults, fed up with the horseplay, start yelling, patience long gone. Dawn breaks on everyone's discomfort.

What do we do? Do we criticize behind the backs of the guilty? Suspicions and gossip fly to and fro like the morning chatter of the birds. Feelings of guilt on the one hand and of not being respected on the other flourish between the participants, the adult chaperones, and the staff. Then the labeling begins to erase the richness of individual personalities.

We return once again to the covenant. It is risky. It makes us vulnerable. The covenant demands that we speak the truth in a spirit of love recognizing our joys, anxieties, embarrassment, and anger. Everyone in the circle, youth or adult, has the right to speak or to remain silent. Some open their hearts and admit their frustration and exhaustion. Tears fall. Some ask for forgiveness while others offer reconciliation. It is hard work to rebuild the trust needed for safe space. We pick up the threads of all we have learned during our mediation and conflict transformation course to knit renewed relationships. The group atmosphere shifts. To build on what we have learned, we must return to the basics: an honest conversation, risking once again to believe and trust. We pass our talking piece, a seashell, around the circle. Everyone listens attentively as Evelyn speaks. As she struggles to translate her thoughts into words, the phrases falter on her lips, but she doesn't give up.

> I am eighteen years old. My mother abandoned me when I was a small child, and my grandparents are caring for me. It is hard for me to put my thoughts together, and

even though I have tried and tried, I have never learned to read or write. How many times I have felt different, marginalized, and confused. How many times I have dreamt of friendship. When I was invited to participate with a group of teenagers from the church in this mediation course, I conquered my fears and joined even though my grandfather did not approve. He reluctantly gave me permission to come to camp on the very night before we left. He didn't sign my permission slip, but said I could come, so I did. I was afraid when the leaders at camp realized I didn't have a signed permission form, but one of the chaperones from my church group said she would be responsible for me. It was against the rules, but the camp staff said they knew somehow I was meant to be here, and they wanted me to stay.

I can't read the songbook; I can't write what I feel in the journal I have made. I have a hard time understanding the instructions, but people are patient with me and I participate in everything.

And in the closing circle, when we were singing, 'The voyage has been a long one, but I have finally arrived,' a girl who has been in my group during camp placed her arm around my shoulders. We are not from the same town; we didn't know each other before taking this course. She is strong, sure of herself, intelligent, happy, capable. We are so different, and yet, for the first time in my life, I have a friend.

The path of peace is not a straight line; it is a path that weaves inside ourselves and out to others. It is a path that takes us backwards to be able to go forward.

QUESTIONS

1. Have you ever participated in a "circle process" where everyone has the opportunity to speak and to be listened to by the group? If so, what do you remember about the experience?
2. What is the difference between agreeing to a community covenant and obeying a set of rules? What do you think a covenant is for, and when is it needed? What do you think the rules are for, and when are they needed?

12

Holy Ground

"'I am the God of your fathers, the God of Abraham, Isaac and Jacob.' Moses trembled with fear and did not dare to look. Then the Lord said to him, 'Take off your sandals, for the place where you are standing is holy ground.'"

ACTS 7:32-33

The youth from the Curicó church had been carefully preparing for the arrival of their international guests for over six months, and the moment had finally arrived. In a special worship service at the end of a week of challenges, misunderstandings, laughter, and learning, they invited the sixteen delegates from the United Church of Christ in Shrewsbury, Massachusetts, to the front of the sanctuary. After words of appreciation and gratitude, the youth from Chile began filing down the aisle to give their new friends the homemade gifts they had created during the past months. The gifts spilled out into the arms of the teenagers from the United States: sandals, lamps, bookends, crocheted doilies, painted tablecloths, dolls, wooden cars, and so many others that soon the floor in front of the altar was covered. I watched the faces of the young guests as the looks of surprise turned to tears and deep-felt emotions.

The next day, as we processed the event, I asked the North American youth what they had felt as their hosts came forward and showered them not only with tangible presents, but with hugs and expressions of love. Their comments reflected the swirling mix of thoughts and feelings: "I stood there with my arms open to receive and felt like I had nothing to give back. I wanted to do something to say thank you, but there was nothing I could do." "I kept thinking that I didn't deserve so much love. I felt so unworthy."

It took the group a few moments to understand that in daring to travel to another country and in humbly and graciously opening their arms to receive, they were participating in a sacred invitation to relationship. As we sat on the floor in a reverent silence, the members of the group realized that they had lived a holy moment; their Chilean sisters and brothers had presented them with a tangible example of the overflowing, abundant, undeserved, and wondrous grace of God.

In the cross-cultural experiences we facilitate at the Shalom Center, people are invited to stretch out their hands, stand together, and walk on a risky pilgrimage to holy ground. The journey is always new and full of surprises, and each turn in the road brings opportunities to grow. It is primarily a spiritual quest. As pilgrims along the path to a deeper understanding of the gospel of Jesus Christ and to a joyous, but respectful, celebration of God's diverse creation, there are pivotal moments where we can no longer turn back to who we were before embarking on the journey. Those who have chosen this path, like Moses before the burning bush in the desert, tread on holy ground. The struggles, confusions, fears, misunderstandings, and discomforts lead step by step to a new dependence on the Holy Spirit and to a broader perspective of who we are in relationship with God as well as others.

Another holy moment in that memorable pilgrimage with the youth from the Shrewsbury church came when we visited a family who live in a small cottage tucked away between the hills of the coastal mountain range of Chile, where they care for a flock of sheep. Under a thorny tree between the house and a small corral, we set a rickety table, the only one available, to celebrate communion. Neither the young Chilean hosts nor the North American guests had ever participated in a communion service outside of a church building or formal worship. The bishop of the Pentecostal Church of Chile and the pastor of the Shrewsbury church consecrated the elements of fresh bread, baked in an outdoor clay oven, and homemade wine. They spoke the familiar words in both English and Spanish with such a harmonious coordination that there was little need of translation. As we served the elements to one another, a gentle breeze suddenly sprang up and the indescribable presence of God was palpably felt by all. Tears of joy and smiles of understanding shone on every face during one of those silences that communicates deeper than words. We knew we were standing on holy ground.

Six months after their visit to Chile, I had the privilege of meeting with this same delegation back in Massachusetts. I was curious to find out if the trip had made any lasting impact on their lives. After a time of answering questions about their many friends, looking at the trip photographs, and laughing or crying with the memories, I asked the group how the experience of traveling to Chile and participating in the partnership between the Pentecostal Church of Chile and the Massachusetts Conference of the UCC had changed their lives. One teenage boy started by remembering that he and his extended family had gathered every year for a traditional New England Thanksgiving meal with all the trimmings. This year, after returning from Chile, he had decided to organize his family to prepare the same meal but to serve it at a local soup kitchen. Then another young woman continued by explaining that every Christmas she had compiled long lists of the presents that she wished to receive. This year, however, she added up the total cost of the items on her list and then asked her parents donate the entire amount to a shelter for the homeless. With a grin stretched across her face, she recalled, "I didn't get a single present for Christmas, and it is the best holiday I have ever had!" One by one, each of the members of the Shrewsbury delegation explained their new sensitivity to people, awareness of global situations, desire to live simpler lifestyles, and intentions in making a difference in their local communities.

The pilgrimage to Chile made these teenagers face one of the basic contradictions of their young lives as North American Christians: Is it possible to enjoy the material abundance so prized by their culture and, at the same time, search humbly for the justice proclaimed by their faith? They had not found any easy answers on the journey; rather they were struggling with new questions. Perhaps it is the questions, born in the intercultural experience, that force us to mature into responsible citizens of the global community. Perhaps is in the recognition of our doubts that we are stripped of our self-reliance and cultural certainty. Perhaps when we recognize how much we need each other, sisters and brothers around the world, then we are ready to accept that divine invitation to take off our shoes and step onto holy ground.

QUESTIONS

1. Have you ever been on a spiritual pilgrimage to a culture different than your own? What did you learn?
2. Why is it important for churches to organize and provide cross-cultural experiences?
3. Can you remember an experience where you felt like you had "stepped into holy space?" In what ways did you change after this experience?

13

The Girl-Butterfly

Do not conform to the pattern of this world, but be
transformed by the renewing of your mind. Then you
will be able to test and approve what God's will is—his
good, pleasing and perfect will.

ROMANS 12:2

Amid the complex interplay of pattern and novelty, the
fluttering of a butterfly's wings in California influences
the weather patterns in Washington, D.C. . . . Love rather
than alienation is essential to reality.

BRUCE G. EPPERLY[1]

María Paz is a butterfly.[2] When she was just a girl she had a
caterpillar's life crawling near the ground and hoping she could
get what she needed without being noticed. She would hide in
a corner at night when she heard her father bellowing down the
block and before he slammed open the door blubbering drunken
nonsense to her mother. She knew that when her mother sent her
away to her grandmother's house, it was because the yelling had
turned to beatings, and she would wait with the anxiety only a
little girl can feel, hoping her mother would call her home soon.

María Paz is a butterfly. Her mother eventually stood up to
her father and forced him to leave. He did, taking every piece of
furniture, the tin roof, and even the front door from their two-room
shack. He has another woman now, and her mother works long
hours as a housekeeper earning barely a couple of dollars a day to
feed and care for her family. She sits and talks with her daughter

---

[1]Bruce G. Epperly in *God's Touch: Faith, Wholeness, and the Healing Miracles of Jesus* (Westminster John Knox Press, 2001).
[2]The names in this story have been changed.

in the evenings when she comes home from work, listening to her stories about school and encouraging her to dream beyond the dirt streets and smells of open sewers.

María Paz is a butterfly. She has two older brothers; one is in jail and the other has moved back to his mother's home with his wife and baby because he has lost his job. María Paz walks an hour to church, Sunday School, youth group meetings, choir and theater practice, and worship because she can't afford to take the local bus, but she is always there, shy and faithful, smiling encouragement to everyone.

Church has been María Paz's cocoon. In the safe, warm embrace of the church community, the molecular structure of her dismal childhood reconfigured into the beautiful woman she was to become. From a frightened and elusive, earthbound creature, there grew one beautiful, airy, and free.

Justin was a foster kid. His father committed suicide, and his mother's drug addiction prevented her from caring for her children. For many years, Justin was bumped from home to home to the point that he refused to learn people's names. Why bother to get close enough to learn someone's name if they weren't going to be around for long? One foster family loved him enough to adopt him, but he just couldn't allow himself to love them back. In his pain, he pulled his hair out, leaving scars and scabs on his soul as well as his scalp. Then one day, the preacher lady offered to take him to a play.

María Paz never dreamt that she would spread her wings and fly to another continent. She was only fifteen when the theater group was invited to bring the sights and sounds of the Pentecostal Church of Chile to the church in the United States. During an evening performance, María Paz noticed a boy sitting in the front row, his eyes wide open with rapt attention and his face radiant with pleasure. Later that night, she heard the boy's story, and she wept as much for him as for herself. They were butterfly tears, not caterpillar ones that burn with powerlessness and discouragement, but tears that wash clean and leave commitment and strength in their place.

María Paz took Justin under her wings as she left and flew back home. She prayed for him at every theater group meeting. She wrote him letters and cards in Spanish, realizing that he could hold them even if he couldn't read them. She asked about him to every person who visited from the United States, hoping someone would know how he was doing. From across the miles of sea and land, she kept faith knowing the weather would change for Justin—faith enough for two.

The next few years were stormy ones for the boy. He was tossed to and fro in the vast ocean of the social service system, and he nearly drowned in the confusion and pain. Like many foster kids, he was in danger of becoming another number in the statistics of those children who don't make it to a safe harbor and are forever lost at sea.

There and back again to the United States, María Paz had learned to fly, and she bravely kept beating her wings when she arrived home. She finished high school and started college. She became the leader of the theater team and kept playing the banjo in the choir. She learned to preach. She made friends with her father's new wife and found ways to encourage her mother and her siblings. Over the years, she never forgot the little boy sitting on the front row whose heart cried out to hers.

Justin is no longer a foster child. He has been adopted by a family that loves him deeply. He is a normal high school boy who dates, plays sports, and thinks about college. Pinned up in a place of honor in his room is a T-shirt with the signatures of the members from a Chilean church theater team and hidden in a box under his bed are the letters written in Spanish that he cannot read. The storm has passed over.

María Paz is a butterfly. The fluttering of her wings has changed the weather patterns in the life of another thousands of miles away. As Bruce G. Epperly would say, *"Love rather than alienation is essential to reality."*

JOURNAL NOTES

The Girl-Butterfly story continues to unfold. María Paz, who is still living with her mother in central Chile, is nearly finished with college and is already teaching in a municipal elementary school where the children have many special needs. Justin is working and has been accepted to a prestigious merchant marine academy. The local newspaper in the town where he lives in the United States recently listed all of the awards he received as he graduated from high school.

QUESTIONS

1. How did María Paz's commitment to Justin help bring about her own healing?

2. Have you heard of other stories where the actions of one person have touched the lives of others far away?
3. There are many ways, through our church connections, in which we can initiate and maintain life-changing relationships with people in other parts of the world: child sponsorship, short-term volunteer opportunities, and sister church partnerships, among others. How might God be calling you to "flutter your wings" and change the weather in another part of the world?

14

"Campo Alegre" Means Happy Field

> For it is by grace you have been saved, through faith—
> and this is not from yourselves, it is the gift of God—not
> by works, so that no one can boast. For we are God's
> handiwork, created in Christ Jesus to do good works,
> which God prepared in advance for us to do.
>
> EPHESIANS 2:8-10

The windshield wipers were busy swishing the rainwater away as we bounced through mud puddles and rocky creek beds. I couldn't believe we were really going to try to make it to Campo Alegre (Happy Field), a commune belonging to a Mapuche[1] reservation where the Pentecostal Church of Chile has a small congregation. I had come south to attend the national conference for pastors, and earlier in the morning when I had seen the sunshine reflecting off the brilliant white cone of the Villarrica volcano, I chose to tag along with the three men planning to make their way out to the country church. Soon after buckling my seatbelt, the volcano disappeared behind the clouds, and the road turned into a gutted, washed out cart track.

The dogs were the first to greet us, barking and chasing the car as we drove up to a house put together with rough boards and a tin roof. After a couple of seconds the faces peeking out the windows disappeared and the door opened. A man ran out to greet us, ushering us one by one under a tattered umbrella to the front porch. My muddy shoes left tracks on the spotless wooden floor. When I was introduced as the "missionary," brother Sergio and

---

[1]The Mapuche people are among the first peoples of southern Chile. There are still many vibrant Mapuche communities that preserve their traditions and language.

sister Viviana could hardly contain their excitement. Sister Viviana took me straight to the kitchen, clasping and unclasping her hands, beaming a smile as warm as the wood fire burning in the stove. In two shakes of a cow's tail (I counted them on the cow in the field just outside the window!), we were settled with the traditional cup of tea and fresh baked bread and beginning to feel right at home.

The conversation, as usual, started light and polite. But, as I have discovered to be true in God's great family, the church, it didn't take long for us to "entrar en confianza" (to trust in one another). Soon I was asking questions about the Mapuche uprisings this year due to the loss of tribal lands. Timber companies and hydroelectric projects had claimed forests that by tradition have belonged to the Mapuches.

"Mapuche means 'children of the earth.' Our land is who we are." Brother Sergio spoke with concern at the rising tide of violence, but also clarified that only a small number of his people supported the aggressive reactions. Most desired a peaceful and fair settlement. When I looked out at his field, I could see the evidence of one of Chile's greatest environmental problems: acute erosion of fertile lands due to overgrazing, deforestation, inappropriate farming practices, and the steep slope toward the sea. Stones popped up all over the field, and the grass was short and patchy in spite of the rainy season. I listened to the rain on the tin roof while he spoke of the severe economic problems his family was facing this year. No one was buying the little wooden key holders and plaques he was making to sell at the market, tourism to the volcano had been slow, and his fields and cows were not producing like they used to. In spite of the difficulties, every word was spiced with love for the land and gratitude to God for the many blessings of family, church, and unexpected guests.

"The rain will stop at twelve noon. It is the shepherd's break to check on the sheep, and you will be able to go see the river and our fields beyond the marsh," said sister Viviana. Sure enough, at 12 o'clock sharp, she set me up with a pair of rubber waders and a baseball cap, and pushed me gently outside. She called from the back door, "Be sure you return in a half-hour since it will start raining again!"

What joy to slosh in puddles with the smell of muddy grass tickling my nose! What fun to wade through a gurgling stream and pick out glistening pebbles! A bull snorted as we crossed the pasture to a bamboo thicket. "This is my sanctuary," said brother Sergio with his eyes misty and a little bit of a croak in his voice.

"Whenever God and I need to talk, I kneel in a clearing in the middle of the thicket. God has never yet failed to answer me there." I could see it was a private kind of place and understood why he didn't invite us inside.

"This is the cow we will sell at the market this year." "This is the marshy area where our commune hopes to set up a salmon pond." "This is the field where we can see the volcano during the day and the stars at night." "Here is a bird's nest. Three eggs means they are recently laid and fresh to eat. Four eggs means leave them to hatch." What a privilege to have the tour of the commune lands with a Mapuche brother as a guide.

In a half-hour we were headed back to the house, just as the wind picked up and the rain began to dot our jackets. Sister Viviana had lugged fresh water from the stream; their well caved in during an earthquake earlier in the year. She also had a sheep tied to the shed with a knife and bowl of water arranged on a nearby crate. Brother Sergio slaughtered the sheep carefully so as to not waste any part of it. Soon the meat was grilling on the fire, along with potatoes boiling in a pot. The table was set with a spotless cloth, patched here and there with tiny stitches, and a mixed match of cups, glasses, and plates. When I asked to use the outhouse, I discovered it to be as clean and orderly as everything else in this home.

In just a few hours, Brother Sergio and Sister Viviana had showered me with gifts: a warm welcome, trust, a tour, lunch, their faith, their stories. I felt honored but so undeserving of their generosity. Ever since I have been a missionary, I have struggled with issues surrounding gifts: giving, receiving, sharing, traditions, rules, when, how, what kind. In Campo Alegre, I faced the dilemma again: My soul was overflowing with their gifts, and I had nothing to give in return. Once more, I experienced grace: a wildly joyous gift given freely with no strings attached. All I had to offer was my desire to be present and my open heart willing to receive. Humbleness and gratitude are prerequisites to experiencing grace, full and running over as that stream dancing with fresh rainwater.

The parting gift shattered my last bit of self-control. Sister Viviana, with eyes brimming and voice trembling, searched my face and chose to trust me with the weight on her soul. Only a week before our visit, the doctors at the main hospital in Temuco had diagnosed her with breast cancer. Chemotherapy was out of the question—too expensive. In a few days, she would be going back to the doctors in hopes of another solution. Even as she wept, her eyes and her voice claimed her faith in the healing power of her Lord. Brother Sergio reached out to hold her tenderly and then broke down himself.

The rain didn't stop, but the clock and the shadows warned us that it was time to go. The three men, brother Sergio, Sister Viviana, and I knelt in the living room to pray, as is the custom when leaving a home belonging to brothers and sisters of the church. One of the men reached out to anoint Sister Viviana's head as he prayed for her healing. She whispered, "My Lord Jesus, let me live." Tears streamed down my face as I pleaded along with her and felt the swirling emotions of sorrow, joy, doubt, and trust. She held my hand, our faith coming together in one prayer.

Sister Viviana held me tightly as we stood in the doorway. "Thank you for visiting my home. Please come back. You will always be welcomed here." I didn't have words to comfort her in return. All I had was a hug and a kiss that welled up from that overflowing cup inside me. The last picture of Campo Alegre imprinted in my mind is that of Brother Sergio and Sister Viviana embracing each other, waving vigorously, and shouting good-byes with tears, raindrops, and grateful smiles shining on their cheeks. I carry their gifts in my heart, as I have once again tasted the pure sweetness of grace.

QUESTIONS

1. What are some of the traditions around hospitality and gift-giving in your culture?
2. What do you and your church believe about praying for miraculous healing?
3. We often think about mission as our responsibility to share what God has given to us with others. How does this story present a different perspective on our mission as followers of Christ?

15

Divine Recycling

Yet the Lord longs to be gracious to you; therefore he
will rise up to show you compassion. For the Lord is a
God of justice. Blessed are all who wait for him!
    People of Zion, who live in Jerusalem, you will weep
no more. How gracious he will be when you cry for
help! As soon as he hears, he will answer you. Although
the Lord gives you the bread of adversity and the water
of affliction, your teachers will be hidden no more; with
your own eyes you will see them. Whether you turn to
the right or to the left, your ears will hear a voice behind
you, saying, "This is the way; walk in it."

Isaiah 30:18-21

Not long ago I visited an area within the city of Concepción
near where the Bío Bío River, the largest river in Chile, flows into the
Pacific Ocean. It is a beautiful place with a new avenue following
the curves of the banks and a river-walk jeweled with green
parks, newly planted trees, and spaces for picnics near modern
playgrounds. From the tiny apartment overlooking the river, I can
hear an occasional boat whistle punctuating the bubbling noise of
families out enjoying the spring weather. How this community has
changed since I first visited nearly ten years ago.

Back then, it was a neighborhood of despair, the land of the
poorest of the poor. Originally, it had been a squatter's community
where homeless people coming into the city looking for jobs
banded together to put roofs over their heads. They used tin, wood,
cardboard, or whatever else they could find in the dump to build
a makeshift shanty on abandoned government property. When
the government tried to evict them from the land, they refused to
leave. They contacted the press and managed to hold on to those

homes they had eked out of nothing. Whenever the river flooded beyond its banks, it washed away the makeshift houses. When the water receded, the people kept coming back.

There still aren't enough jobs in Concepción, Chile's second largest city. Back then, unemployment was even higher. Violence was never far from the front door. On my first visit, a murdered body was found on a street corner. No one knew who the person was, and the police dared not enter the area until the following morning. The body lay in the street overnight; no one would touch it because they were afraid of getting involved. The dreaded hantavirus ran rampant here, fed by the poverty and carried by the rats. Even the dust where the rats have been can bear the deadly disease. Mothers had to guard their babies in their cradles for fear that a rat might run through the room leaving a trail of death.

During that first visit, the church people told me they were worried because the city government had determined it was time for the whole "población" (a barrio or poor neighborhood in Chile) to be torn down, ridding the community of vermin and disease. The people speculated about what would happen to them. They suspected that those who had enough money would be able to live on the same land in brand new government-built housing. Most people who had a little extra would never have chosen to live in the "población" in the first place. Would the people who didn't have the money to pay for a new apartment be pushed out onto the streets? This tiny apartment with running water and cheery curtains, overlooking the banks of the Bío Bío, belongs to a family who once lived in a cardboard-walled and tin-roofed shack. They are longtime members of the Pentecostal Church of Chile. With laughter and tears, and the still fresh amazement of the radical changes that have come over their neighborhood, they speak of the slow but steady transformation from streets run by drug lords to kites, bikes, and soccer games. I remembered a story told to me by two women from Massachusetts who visited the church before the changes occurred and stayed in this community for a week.

"It was Sunday morning and the church school recitation and songs had ended. It was about time to go home, but a hush descended over the congregation. We knew something important was about to happen. A man who sat in the back of the church began to speak. He spoke sitting in his pew, as if he were not worthy to come forward. His face was young, but his bearing was like that of an old man, as if he had seen too much of life already. He told his story through a translator, so we know we did not get the whole story. But this is what we understood:

> I was a bad man. When I was in prison, I was the worst of the worst. If I pointed to a man and said, ‹Die,› then someone from my gang would do the dirty work. I was the one who decided who would live and who would die. I was the leader because I was the toughest. I didn't care about anyone, not even myself. I had no softness in my heart.
>
> Toward the end of my sentence, I got into a knife fight with the head of the other gang in prison. I had 17 stab wounds, any one of which could have killed me. As I lay in the murky place between life and death, an angel appeared to me. She told me, ‹Stop living this life. Turn away from it and live a new life.› When I became conscious again, the hospital, the doctors, and the prison didn't seem real anymore. Only the angel was real. So I changed my life and became a new man.
>
> Today, I collect trash: the rubbish that others have thrown out, those things that are discarded, of no use to anyone. I find something of value in them. I make art from them.

"Then the man, whose name was Ricardo, stood up and opened a bag. Out of it, he pulled a beautifully carved and painted mask, fashioned from a discarded pipe. In the one countenance of the mask there were three faces. Ricardo finished by saying:

> See in this rubbish the face of God. When I was trash, thrown away, of no use to anyone, God saw something of value in me and salvaged me. This is my job now, to salvage rubbish into art and be a grateful witness of God's love."

The women from Massachusetts were given a glimpse into a vision of something that had not yet happened. One of them wrote, "Then I knew the neighborhood of despair was really a neighborhood of hope. People came to this modest little church and discovered something of value in themselves and each other. They gave testimonies, sang songs, and cried rivers of tears while laughing and clapping with the joy of it all. Something extraordinary had happened that day. I had laid eyes on the face of the resurrected Christ still among us, alive, active and powerful."

Here I was, looking out the window over the place of transformation. The tiny congregation that was a light in the middle of the darkness continues to be a beacon of God's life-giving power. I have heard that Ricardo is now curator of an art museum. Like Ricardo, the whole community has been transformed. God makes no garbage but takes the trash in our lives and works it over until we are molded into the masterpieces God intended, unique reflections of God's very self. Our God is, after all, the garbage-collecting master of recycled art.

QUESTIONS

1. This is a story of the transformation of an individual as well as a community. Do you know of any other examples where individuals and communities have been transformed by God's love?
2. Ricardo found a place in church to pursue his art after he got out of jail. What do you think are the characteristics of a church that welcomes and encourages people like Ricardo to fulfill their dreams?
3. What do you think of the image of God as the "garbage-collecting master of recycled art"? Do you agree or disagree with this image of God? What is your preferred image of God?

16

Bottles for the Bathroom

Do two walk together unless they have agreed to do so?

Amos 3:3

Viviana and her husband, Carlos, moved to Talca, the same city where I live, when he was sent to become the new pastor of the church. The congregation, a little over twenty years old, needed to recharge its spiritual batteries and embrace a new vision of God's calling.

The only bathrooms at the church were two tiny dark closets in the basement. Pastor Carlos and Pastora Viviana decided that one way to energize the congregation would be to build new bathrooms together.

The people of the congregation responded with skepticism. Where would they get the $2 million pesos (about $4,000) for the bathrooms? Pastora Viviana thought that if the project had a jumpstart, the people would soon join in by giving what they could even before they had faith in the completion of the project. She organized the women of the church, and they began to collect plastic bottles for recycling. Soon, the whole church was picking up bottles on the street and asking their neighbors for more. They collected all through the summer, and by the end of two months, there were one hundred large sacks of crushed beverage bottles sitting in the parsonage's postage-stamp-size backyard. The day came to take the sacks to the recycling center, and the members of the congregation enthusiastically volunteered, taking several trips in an old pickup and a cart.

On the following Sunday, Pastora Viviana reported to the congregation that they had raised the first $50,000 pesos (one hundred dollars) for the new bathrooms. It was the spark the congregation needed. Small offerings began to trickle in. Different members of the congregation worked together on the weekends to dig the foundations and lay the bricks. Little by little, always with just enough money to buy the building supplies that would be needed the next weekend, the bathrooms began to take shape. Enthusiasm followed behind the visible evidence of what had been a pipe dream to some. The tile floors, aluminum partitions, and bathroom fixtures sparkled on the day of the inauguration thanks to the natural light coming in through high windows.

As the miracle of the pleasant bathrooms has taken shape, another subtler miracle has unfolded. The congregation has a new spirit. There is a sense of community and cooperation, and a new desire to serve God and others outside the walls of the church building. Now the members of the congregation are talking about starting an environmental education club with the children of the community and adding on to the church so as to accommodate a wider outreach to those in need.

The project began with Pastora Viviana's vision and the collecting of bottles. When I spoke to her about writing this story, Pastora Viviana told me to share her words: "Give and receive all of the love that you can. In every tiny act, God is teaching us to love and to accept the love of others. God has a special purpose for every single woman and has also the perfect timing to bring about that purpose. Live each day loving, and God's purpose will sprout inside of you, growing out in blessing to many others."

QUESTIONS

1. What projects do you know that started with something as simple as collecting plastic bottles for recycling and turned into blessings for many people?
2. Why do you think this practical, down-to-earth project inspired the congregation to work together?
3. What kind of project would bring together and inspire the members of your community or congregation?

17

We Are All Related

By this everyone will know that you are my disciples, if you love one another.

JOHN 13:35

Maria stayed home with her mother who was ill and did not go to church that day. Her mother was resting in the bedroom when Maria noticed the orange and red light flickering in the skylight near sunset. At the same time she peered through the window to discover the next-door neighbor's house completely engulfed in flames, the people across the street began to scream a warning at the front gate of their small wood-frame and brick house. Maria and her mother fumbled to find the gate key to let them in. Acquaintances and friends from several blocks around jumped over the eye-level metal bars of the fence and began pulling everything Maria's family owned from their house including the refrigerator, the beds, and even jumbled heaps of clothes from the clothesline. By the time the firemen arrived and doused the flames, the house was almost empty. The roof of their home was a charred mess and water dripped down the walls and pooled on the cement floor, but most of their belongings suffered no smoke or water damage.

The Harvest Day worship on May 1 is my favorite church service in the Pentecostal Church of Chile. On this day, we celebrate the abundance of God's creation as farmers bring the first and best fruits to the church altar, including everything from chickens, ducks, and goats to onions, apples, and potatoes. Bakers, craftsmen, tailors, carpenters, and popcorn vendors walk down the aisle with their offerings, too. In the middle of the joyous cacophony of choir music, excited children, and squawking ducks, my friend Richard searched me out and shouted above the din that he needed the keys to the Shalom Center's pickup truck. "The Ramos's house is on fire," he exclaimed. I had a hard time hearing him, so he didn't offer any details before running off to help carry the loads of furniture the neighbors had rescued from the curb in front of the house to the nearby home of another church family. A few minutes later, there was a pause in the middle of the worship service to pray for the Ramos family with the invitation to give a special offering.

One of the elders drove me to the Ramos's house after the Harvest Day worship ended since the pickup truck had not been returned. Maria said one relief-filled word as she stepped toward me, her arms open for my embrace: "¡Tía!" ("aunt" in Spanish). I gathered her family into a circle in the waterlogged living room with the acrid stench of burnt wood sticking in my nostrils. As we prayed, the Ramos family lifted their hands, weeping in praise and thanksgiving for lives spared. Two of their neighbors died in the fire next door.

By the time the winter rains began some weeks later, volunteers from the church had rebuilt the Ramos's house. It was roomier and painted in cheery colors. The neighbors, who had helped rescue the belongings, returned each item once the house was ready, even the $5,000-peso bill (about ten dollars) that had been lying on top of the refrigerator. I spent an afternoon hauling beds and clean clothes (another neighbor washed and ironed their ash-flecked, rumpled garments) back to their house in the pickup truck. Maria›s mother still has nightmares about the fire, but her family has been accompanied every step along the way to spiritual and physical recovery by the women and men of the church. We are family, "en las buenas y en las malas" (in the good times and in the bad times), as they say in Chile.

Those rains came without the cold temperatures due in winter. In Chile, this combination of rain and warmer temperatures spells disaster. The precipitation that should accumulate as snow and ice on the folds of the Andes Mountains runs downhill filling rivers, scraping away the topsoil, and tumbling trees and boulders in its path. That year, the Mataquito River, its banks denuded of trees that would have absorbed some of the water, turned into a swirling chocolate brown torrent that swept into the village of Licanten, a few miles from the coast of the Maule Region. Within a few hours, the pastor of the Pentecostal Church of Chile in Licanten called the central office of the church to report that the water was climbing up to the second story of the boxlike house where he and his wife were attempting to escape from the flood. There hadn't been time to evacuate. Two days later, with much of the town still seven feet under water and none of the municipal services restored, I received a phone call from a friend at the regional CONAMA[1] office. The emergency response teams from this office had been working nonstop throughout the flood, and her voice was weary and strained. "Where are the Christians in this time of crisis?" she asked me accusingly. The Pentecostals in Chile are often criticized by the wider society for apparently showing little concern when there are practical needs in this earthly life and concentrating mainly on the life to come. I had no answer.

But the church family did. The next Sunday, in worship services throughout the country, people took off their winter coats, necklaces, new shoes, and even wedding rings and placed them in offering plates and at the altar. My friend called me back on Monday. "Three trucks and a half-dozen cars have arrived from the Pentecostal Church of Chile filled with goods, and the local church pastor will be sharing it all with the wider community!" One of the trucks was filled with onions, potatoes, and other food from the offerings of the farmers during the Harvest Day worship service that had been kept in storage for just such a need. The other trucks were loaded with clothes, shoes, refrigerators, and stoves. This time I did have an answer for my friend at the Conama office: "See, we are all family, after all!"

We *are* all related. In the Pentecostal Church of Chile, we call each other "sister" and "brother," and though we are not related by blood, we are all part of the same spiritual family bound together by God's love. Children refer to adults that they particularly admire and respect as "aunt" or "uncle." As in most families, there is plenty of petty gossip, sibling rivalry, and indiscreet snooping, but when there is a need, all these are overshadowed by solidarity, sacrificial giving, and love.

QUESTIONS

1. Does your church have a special thanksgiving or harvest day service? How is it similar or different from the service in the Pentecostal Church of Chile?
2. Does your church help families who have lost their homes in a fire or a flood? How is your help similar or different from what the Pentecostal Church of Chile offers?
3. Can you think of other experiences in which you were reminded that we are all related as God's children?

---

[1]Chile's equivalent of the Environmental Protection Agency

18

Do Hungry People Ring Your Doorbell?

"Then the King will say to those on his right, 'Come, you who are blessed by my Father; take your inheritance, the kingdom prepared for you since the creation of the world. For I was hungry and you gave me something to eat, I was thirsty and you gave me something to drink, I was a stranger and you invited me in, I needed clothes and you clothed me, I was sick and you looked after me, I was in prison and you came to visit me.'"

MATTHEW 25:34-36

Do hungry people ring your doorbell? This is a common occurrence in my life. Last week, an elderly woman rang the doorbell right at dusk. It was cold out, and I ran to answer it, thinking it was one of the girls who had forgotten her keys. "Would you have something you could give me to eat?" she asked me politely. Our pantry was nearly empty, because Acsa, the nursing student who lives with me, had not yet been to the store for the week. I found a box of macaroni and cheese and took it to the gate. She received the box with heartfelt thanks.

A second after I closed the door, the doorbell rang again. "Can you tell me how to cook this?" asked the same lady. "I don't know how to read," she added. I read the instructions on the box for her.

Yesterday it was right after lunch. We had guests and no leftovers. I answered the door when the bell rang. This time it was a young man with dreadlocks. He looked confused when I asked, in the traditional way, "¿En qué le puedo servir?" (how might I be of service to you?). He could not look directly at me as he mumbled, "What can I do? I am hungry." I asked him to wait a minute. Acsa helped me prepare a cheese sandwich, a cup of hot tea, and an apple. Again he did not look at me as I gave him the food, but he said "thank you" softly and placed the sandwich, the cup, and the apple in an old paint bucket and walked away.

I rarely see the same people twice, and have often wondered if someone has put a secret mark on our house or if people work their way through the whole neighborhood until they get to ours. The answer came to me last year, on an icy day, when an effeminate, barefoot, toothless, shaggy-haired young man rang the doorbell. He frightened Carolina, my other housemate, and at the same time sparked her compassion. She called me to the door. "I am hungry," he stated in a childlike voice, "and I want to go home." I opened the gate and went and sat next to him on the curb. He told me his long sad story of abuse and loneliness. Carolina prepared some food as I listened. I gave him the five dollars he said he needed for the bus home. We got him a warm pair of socks and a jacket, too. He smiled and exclaimed excitedly, "I just knew that at this house I would find someone who loves God! I can see in your eyes that you do." I guess God has marked our house. Has God marked yours?

QUESTIONS

1. Do people, either spiritually or physically hungry, catch your attention or "ring your doorbell"?
2. What is your first reaction when you come across someone who is begging?
3. In Chile there are no food pantries and few free lunch programs for adults who are hungry, though the government schools do offer lunch to students. In considering the big picture, what might be some of the problems created by giving food or clothing to people who ring the doorbell?
4. Do you think the missionary should keep giving people food at her doorstep, or do you think she should think of another solution to this problem? What could be a realistic solution?

19

The Scarecrow and God

Every good and perfect gift is from above, coming down from the Father of the heavenly lights, who does not change like shifting shadows.

JAMES 1:17

We had agreed to fix up the yard together. Acsa, the nursing student who lives at the Gathering Point[1] with me, wanted a small herb garden, and I wanted to get rid of the weeds and prepare a compost bin. We went to the garden store together and decided on a large trash can for the compost. Then we lugged two big bags of mulch and picked out baby mint, oregano, cilantro, and ruda plants. In the corner of the garden store, there were cute little handmade scarecrows crafted on pointed sticks to place in the garden. "Let's take a scarecrow!" Acsa begged. "No," I said firmly. "We are already over our budget." For the next couple of weeks, Acsa kept reminding me of the scarecrow as we worked on the yard and garden. "Wouldn't a little scarecrow look fun here?" she cajoled, trying to convince me. It reminded me of Dr. Seuss's *Green Eggs and Ham*: "I do not like them, Sam-I-am. I do not like green eggs and ham!"

On a bitter winter evening last week, the smoke from the wood-burning fireplaces covered the streets of our neighborhood with a foggy blanket, making it dark early. The doorbell rang. When I answered, a middle-aged woman stood facing me, shivering in the cold, lips blue. "I have kitchen towels for sale," she offered. "No thanks," I answered, "we don't need any today." "Wait!" she exclaimed when I began to shut the door. "I also have these cute little handmade scarecrows for sale." As I paid for the scarecrow, the lady's face lit up. It was her last sale of the day; now she could go

---

[1]The Shalom Center office in the city of Talca.

home and feed her children. A little later, Asca came home from the university and was overjoyed! "You bought the scarecrow for me!"

I am not sure why a scarecrow for our garden was so important that God had to send one directly to my door, but I guess that is the mysterious way God has of preparing a blessing long before we are aware of it ourselves. The street vendor was blessed, Acsa was blessed, and I was blessed by their joyous reception of the blessing. "Thank you! Thank you, Sam-I-am!"

QUESTIONS

1. Do you think that God has a sense of humor? What are some of the things that make God laugh?
2. Has God ever sent you an unexpected blessing that made you laugh?
3. Do you think that a sense of humor can be an important part of resilience?

20

What Is in a Name?

And even the very hairs of your head are all numbered.
So don't be afraid; you are worth more than many
sparrows.

Matthew 10:30-32

It happened twice after the same worship service, one right
after the other. If it had happened just once, I might have doubted
it was a message from God, but twice? God was reminding me of
the importance of learning and remembering someone's name.

Manuel approached me after the benediction. A well-dressed
lawyer who recently passed the bar exam in Chile, he was carrying
his young daughter tenderly in his arms, and he wanted me to meet
her. Then he said, "I have been meaning to tell you something for a
long time. I remember the first time we met, seventeen years ago.
It was during an open-air evangelism campaign. I was a young
teenager full of doubts about my faith and about continuing in
church. You asked me my name. I told you 'Manuel,' and you never
forgot. Every single time we met after that, you called me by my
name even though there were dozens of other young people in the
church. If I was important enough to you for you to remember my
name, I thought maybe I was important to God, too. We haven't
seen each other very much over the years, but thanks for always
remembering my name. It has meant so much to me."

I am not particularly good at remembering names. Some people
will tell you they have had to introduce themselves to me three or
four times before I remember who they are. Even though I know
it is very important for each of us to be called by name and that I
should strive to remember the names of the people I meet, I also
know my mind is feeble. I have to recognize that usually the Holy
Spirit brings a name into my mind, but sometimes I am just too
busy to pay attention.

Another young man, poorly dressed and with the air of the mountain countryside about him, stood off to one side patiently waiting as I finished talking to Manuel. When I turned to greet him, he took a step back and then asked me, "Do you remember who I am?" I started flipping through my mental card files and came up with a blank. "I am from the little church called Palmera de Cordillería (Mountain Palms)." No bells rang. Then, after a pause, a quiet, earthshaking voice like the whisper to Elijah on the mountainside, spoke a memory into my mind. "Wait!" I exclaimed. "Don't tell me! I know you! You are DAVID!" His face lit up like a thousand suns and his eyes filled with tears. "¡Sí!" he answered. "¡Soy yo!" I took both his hands into mine and asked him how he was doing. "There is so much to tell you," he answered. Then he saw the others also waiting to greet me. "But God is with me and I am doing well."

Others were waiting, and I remembered that the same thing had happened when David was a child. I had visited Palmera de Cordillería with Bishop Ulises Muñoz of the Pentecostal Church of Chile fifteen or sixteen years ago when I was helping to set up the Sunday School program in the Curicó Church. Back then, the bishop had told me that the leader of this daughter church was opposed to any new ideas or programs. The bishop preached, and I shared the children's sermon. The children had stood in the greeting line along with the adults, and one boy, about ten years old, informed me when he shook my hand, "My name is David." "Just like David in the Bible," I answered. "Do you remember who David was?" I asked, but before he could answer the adults pushed him on so others could greet me. David slipped back in the line, and when it was his turn again, he said, "Wasn't David one of Jesus' disciples?" I smiled and said, "Wait here beside me a minute. When I finish saying good-bye to everyone we will talk." I sat down next to David and told him the story of David and Goliath, about David and Jonathan, and how David had been king of Israel. He listened open-mouthed and eyes wide. When there was no one left in the sanctuary but the bishop and the leader, I called them over and asked them to listen. "David," I asked, "Have you ever been to Sunday School?" "What is Sunday School?" he replied. "Would you like for your church to have Sunday School?" I asked after explaining what it would be like and what he would learn. "Oh yes!" he exclaimed. The bishop turned to the leader and stated emphatically with no room to argue, "We will be starting Sunday School in this church!"

Since that brief introduction so long ago, I had only seen David one other time. He was fifteen or sixteen, and that time he had greeted me with, "I know all about King David now!" Ten more years passed. Even if I could have remembered what he looked like as a child or a teen, he was a grown man now. "I wanted so much to see you and say thank you," he said. I kept holding his hands as he looked into my eyes. "Thank you for remembering me. My heart is bursting with joy!" He hugged me, and with the next person wanting to greet me impatiently stepping closer, I said to David, "Please look for me again at the next church gathering when we are both in Curicó. I want to hear your story." He smiled broadly and nodded, turned away, and disappeared into the crowd.

What is in a name? Recognition, relationship, hope, and transformation. With two very different young men, one right after the other, the Holy Spirit reminded me of just how much is in a name.

QUESTIONS

1. Do you usually remember people's names? Do you have a special method for remembering them?
2. How important is it to you for people to remember your name?
3. What is the relationship of our names to our sense of dignity or self-worth?
4. How does it make you feel to know God not only knows your name but even knows the number of hairs on your head?

21

Heavenly Treasures

Do not store up for yourselves treasures on earth, where
moths and vermin destroy, and where thieves break
in and steal. But store up for yourselves treasures in
heaven, where moths and vermin do not destroy, and
where thieves do not break in and steal. For where your
treasure is, there your heart will be also.

MATTHEW 6:19-21

Everything was gone! We were at a quaint little artisans market
in a "safe" part of Santiago, the Chilean capital. The two men from
the Pentecostal Church of Chile had gone inside to let me know
that they had bought all the fixings for sandwiches so we could
have a picnic in the park. A moment later, I walked out to my little
van to get lunch ready for the five women who were visiting us
from the United States. It took me a full minute to realize my van
had been wiped clean. All of the luggage and my computer, which
I had brought to the city for repairs, had been stolen.

How I regretted using that Bible text from Matthew 6 about
treasures in heaven at orientation. We had sat around the altar on
the day they had arrived and discussed what Jesus had meant about
storing our treasures in heaven. It was a theoretical discussion, not
one that I had planned on experiencing!

What exactly were these earthly treasures now gone? Each of
the five women represented a congregation in the United States,
and they were in Chile visiting their "sister churches." The bags
were filled with precious handmade gifts, tokens of friendship, dirty
clothes, Bibles, urgently needed medication, and a few plane tickets.
One of the guests was under 18 years old, and required a special
letter from the Chilean consulate in the United States to be able to
travel back out of Chile without her parents. My computer had on
its hard drive the files of all of the Christian Education materials,
the books that we had written for the Sunday School program,

and most of my digital photos. With our earthly treasures neatly packed into the back of my little van, we had traveled to Santiago stopping at the artisans market on the way to the airport. That was when the warning, "Don't store up treasures on earth!" ceased to be just a theological concept.

We called the police. When they came, they questioned me separately from the two men from the church who were driving the vehicles, implying that it had been an inside job. God's lesson about the little value of "stuff" was to be taught in a thorough way. After my frustration at talking to the police who did not want to hear my explanation of the situation, I walked around the van to reassure our guests. I found the five United Church of Christ women, those "frozen chosen" New Englanders, holding hands in a circle. They were praying, and from that moment, my fear, anger, and indignation dissipated.

The police called to me again. A new officer, with more rank, had shown up. He turned out to be from Curicó, the same town where the Pentecostal Church of Chile has its central offices. Once I explained we were from the church, he quickly took charge and clarified the situation with professionalism and courtesy. While we filed the police report, those five American women stood outside the police station and recited Psalm 121 while standing before the snow-covered Andes Mountains. "I lift up my eyes to the mountains—/ where does my help come from? / My help comes from the Lord, / the Maker of heaven and earth." (Psalm 121:1-2). Next we went to the Chilean pharmacy to replace the stolen medication without a prescription. The police officer went with us and explained the situation to an understanding and helpful pharmacist. We could plainly see that our hearts and treasures were safest in God's hands, when the only parking spot for eight blocks around the airline office was right across the street teeming with traffic. It was just the right size for the nine-passenger van. Even in the cheerless offices of Interpol, we had no problem getting a letter of safe-passage for an unaccompanied minor.

We never recovered any of the luggage nor the computer. However, I had just made a backup of all the information, except the pictures, the week before. Then, within a month after the theft, the sisters and brothers of the Curicó church took up an offering to buy me a new computer. That offering covered the cost of one better suited to the growing needs of my ministry. The computer is a tangible reminder that the true treasure is not the machine, but God›s love shining through God's people.

At the airport, we broke into peals of laughter when a confused ticket agent asked the group to put their luggage on the scale. Once they were checked in, we headed to the airport chapel where we sat in a tight circle talking and praying. "I am grateful no one was hurt." "I hope that my Bible will bless someone else." "God be with the people who did this, whatever their needs may be." "Today I just let go and let God." "The treasures in my heart given to me by my Chilean sisters and brothers can never be stolen." "I felt cared for." "Peace."

Nearly seven years later, one of the five women from Massachusetts drove me to a church in the United States where I was to do a presentation. Shortly after returning home from Chile, she accepted the call she had long felt and refused. She entered seminary, graduated, and now is in full-time parish ministry. That last day in Chile was the turning point of her life. Each of the other four women also discovered their lives taking a different track after this experience.

The treasures I cherish from that day are tucked away in the relationships: God›s protection and care for details placed in the hands of a friendly policeman; God's people putting their faith to work in the least likely places and moments; the church community responding with practical evidence of love. I hope I have learned the lesson God intended to teach us that day, and that I will keep my treasures in my heart and not in my possessions.

QUESTIONS

1. How would you react if you had your belongings stolen while on a trip to another country?
2. Have you ever felt that God took a particular biblical truth and allowed you to experience it in some tangible way?
3. Why is it difficult to maintain a healthy perspective in regard to our earthly treasures?
4. How do we avoid buying into a consumer culture that overemphasizes our earthly treasures?
5. What might be the "treasures in heaven" that the Bible says we should be storing up?

22

Jesus Washed My Hands

When he had finished washing their feet, he put on his
clothes and returned to his place. "Do you understand
what I have done for you?" he asked them. "You call
me 'Teacher' and 'Lord,' and rightly so, for that is what
I am. Now that I, your Lord and Teacher, have washed
your feet, you also should wash one another's feet. I
have set you an example that you should do as I have
done for you.

JOHN 13:12-15

I can almost feel the cold mountain water even now as I
remember filling the black buckets moments before the final work
period at the Shalom Center. It had been a difficult week. The
Chilean kids who came to the Conpaz ("With Peace") camp had
never been in the mountains or with foreigners before, but they
behaved wonderfully: welcoming and enthusiastic. However, I
did not feel connected to the group of teenagers from the United
States. In fact, at times during that week I felt used, discounted, and
rejected. I blamed myself: *I have too many other things on my mind; I
didn't prepare well enough for them; I am too distant from the youth from
the United States to understand their needs.* I got angry: *I have opened
my home and my life's work with little sign of appreciation,* and then
judgmental: *the Chilean kids have been so loving and accepting and the
kids from the United States so self-centered and arrogant.* I was angry,
hurt, and exhausted, but I chose not to lose faith.

Is there such a thing as a disconnected soul? One that is so
dislocated, isolated, or independent that it has no bridge, no fallen
log along the way, to span the gap to another soul? I wonder about
this now, as I reflect back on the week with those teenagers from
the United States—whether or not the dominant culture there is
raising a generation of disconnected souls unable to bring into
healing relationships the balance of needs and gifts, courtesy and

graciousness, collectivity and independence. The foundation for connecting is humility, recognizing our need to give and receive such basics as bread, water, love, and encouragement along life's way. With humility we acknowledge that we need experienced guides to lead us around the dangers on the path. Connecting is a risky way to travel. It means becoming vulnerable over and over at every new encounter with pilgrims unknown. It requires listening, stopping for meals, and "sobremesa," long chats over the table after the meal is finished. To connect is to enter into a community of vagabonds, some ragged and travel worn, others blindly lost, but all tramping and trying to find their way through life.

At the end of the week, the staff, with towels hung over their shoulders, carried the buckets I filled into the circle. One by one, we washed the hands of the youth, Chilean and American alike, blessing their palms and fingers to serve others and then inviting them to take up the buckets and towels and do the same for their new friends. Tenderness spilled out, as fresh and crystalline as the water, when the youth knelt before each other and gently washed and blessed each other's hands. At that moment, I knew how Jesus might have felt when he told the disciples to do the same after he had washed their feet.

A teenage girl from the United States knelt before me, took my hands, and scooped the cool water over them. As she patted my hands dry with the towel, she thanked me and blessed my ministry at the Shalom Center. When her eyes met mine, I understood that we had both put aside our differences, recognizing with humility that God had been at work inside and among us all week. I heard God speak to me in her voice, and I felt Jesus himself had washed my hands with hers.

JOURNAL NOTES

After I told this story to a church group in the United States, a woman shared a childhood memory with me. She remembered that a missionary to Egypt had come to visit her church when she was five or six years old. She could not remember what the missionary said, but there had been an Egyptian meal. Before the meal, the missionary led the participants in a hand-washing ritual. The child was so deeply moved by the ritual that when she grew up, she dedicated herself to helping people from different cultures understand each other. Many years later, as she told me about this memory triggered by my story, she reaffirmed her commitment to reaching out to people across language and cultural barriers. This for me is another of the complex and multilayered connections in storytelling.

QUESTIONS

1. What do you remember about the story where Jesus washed his disciples' feet? How were the disciples changed, or what did they learn in experiencing this ritual?
2. Have you ever participated in a hand- or foot-washing ritual? What did you feel or what do you remember about the experience?
3. If you, or other members of your group or church, have never participated in a hand- or foot-washing ritual, think of an appropriate time and place to experience such a ritual. In organizing and creating the ritual, remember that effective rituals involve the senses, have layers of meaning, often include music, use concrete objects and actions, and flow from the specific to the general, from the loss or pain to renewal, hope, and commitment.

23

Dignity in a Shoelace

Be strong and very courageous. Be careful to obey all the law my servant Moses gave you; do not turn from it to the right or to the left, that you may be successful wherever you go.

Joshua 1:7

In a little beauty parlor where the pungent smells of hair products assailed my senses as much as the whirring of hairdryers, I listened to her story. The testimony began like that of thousands of others who take up the painful journey from the county to the city in search of work and new opportunities. As I looked at her that day, I imagined that at some crossroads or stop along the way, her life twisted unexpectedly onto a different path. I wanted to know how she became the successful owner of her own small business, escaping poverty and beating seemingly insurmountable odds. She continued her story, speaking to the gentle rhythm of the clicking of her scissors.

"My life dawned slowly like the winter sun on the volcanoes that dip their skirts into the rivers and lakes. My mother died a few days after my birth, and my father left me with an aunt. I never saw him again.

"I grew up with the slap of the icy mountain wind on my face and shaped by the lack of love; my dreams fell like seeds on rocky soil where they died before sprouting. The sun was the only shawl I had when I would go out to explore the fields. I hugged the trees to imagine myself loved, and nature was my only childhood comfort. The lambs born in the spring kissed me, and the birds sang to lift my spirits. In my own quiet way, I basked in the afternoons painted in pinks and violets of the sky, snow, and water. The beauty helped me escape my less-than-beautiful reality.

"In that backwoods part of the country, the only opportunity available to a teenage orphan was to marry and have children. My two oldest daughters were born in the lonely sheepherder's hut where I went to live with my husband, without any medical or family care, but we survived. It was the blizzard, called a 'white earthquake,' that nearly killed us—gone were the lambs, and with them, our future. My husband and I took the girls and traveled to the city. He sought work while I hunted for hope.

"We arrived at an illegal land grab on a large vacant lot outside the limits of the capital, and we made ourselves a shelter of cardboard and plastic sheets we found in a dump. I walked the streets swallowing saliva and shame, hunting for food to feed my daughters. Pride would not let me beg; hunger would not let me sleep.

"One day, as I was crossing the traffic-choked main avenue of the city, with my four-year-old daughter hanging from one hand and the two-year-old from the other, both of their dirty faces lined with tears, I felt the despair eating me alive. I was eight months pregnant, my belly bulging under my oil-speckled apron. I had been rummaging through the garbage. I am sure we didn't smell very nice.

"There on the sidewalk, in the confusion of street noise and car exhaust, an older gentleman with graying hair, a nice suit and tie, and a leather briefcase, approached me. At first, I ignored him, my head down to cover my suspicious eyes. When he came directly toward me, I became fearful.

"'Excuse me,' he said in a softly refined voice, 'your shoelace is untied.' I hadn't noticed because, at this point in my pregnancy, I couldn't even see my own feet. 'You might trip,' he continued. 'Allow me.' The gentleman knelt down before me, smiled at my daughters, and firmly tied my shoelace. He stood and took his leave by saying, 'I hope you have a good day, madam.'

"I raised my head and stood up tall. I was no longer an insignificant dot in the mass of humanity traveling the streets of the city. This small gesture refocused my vision of myself. Never before had anyone shown me such respect and esteem. Never before had I felt I was of value. As that man knelt before me on the sidewalk and tied my shoelace, I knew for the first time in my life that I had dignity and was worthy of care and concern.

"On that same day, I began to beg until I was able to buy a pair of hair-cutting scissors. Then I cut hair right out on the curb of a busy street corner. Eventually, I was able to buy a chair. Later I rented a tiny shop near the corner until I bought my own place. I worked hard. Finally, I sold that place and moved to this new city. It has taken many years, but now I have two beauty parlors in different parts of town and all of my children have gone to college."

The hairdresser looked at me through the reflection of the mirror as she touched up my bangs, and with conviction she concluded her story. "This is my dream for my country: that all women be treated with dignity; that even the poorest woman might discover, as I did one day when a rich man tied my shoe, that no matter who we are, we are worthy of respect and honor."

QUESTIONS

1. How would you define the word "dignity" in relation to this story?
2. How does restoring our own dignity as well as the dignity of others change how we see ourselves and how we behave?
3. Think of the rich man in the story. What are some of the simple things we can do each day to uplift the dignity of others?

HEALING
COURAGE

*Women knitting and praying during the prayer
shawl retreat at the Shalom Center shortly after
the 2010 earthquake in central Chile.*

24

The Comfort of a Prayer Shawl

Praise be to the God and Father of our Lord Jesus
Christ, the Father of compassion and the God of all
comfort, who comforts us in all our troubles, so that
we can comfort those in any trouble with the comfort
we ourselves receive from God. For just as we share
abundantly in the sufferings of Christ, so also our
comfort abounds through Christ.

2 CORINTHIANS 1:3-5

The knitting needles clicked rhythmically. Gathered around
a poolside patio table enjoying the sun and a few moments of
quiet reflection apart from the rush of lives overcharged with
responsibilities and needs, we watched as the knots and yarn grew
into a soft, fuzzy, blue, red, and purple shawl. The elderly ladies
in the women's group at the Leominster United Church of Christ
in Massachusetts had started working on the shawl with special
prayers for the missionary who would receive it. Now their pastor
was finishing the shawl in my presence, while a group of women
prayed for God to bless me with wisdom, grace, peace, and comfort
as I returned to Chile to continue my service as a missionary with
Global Ministries.

So the shawl traveled to the Southern Hemisphere. It was
draped across the foot of my bed all through the winter and
accompanied me on long bus rides to workshops. It brought me
comfort on many nights as I curled up in front of the fireplace to
read, pray, or simply enjoy a moment of solitude.

Then Pablo died. He was the eighteen-year-old son of my dear
friend, Rebeca. God brought Rebeca and me together the second
month after I arrived in Chile. We sat next to each other at a meal
during a gathering of church leaders, strangers but sister spirits
just waiting to meet. Long after everyone else had left the room, we
opened our souls, poured out our dreams and hopes, and sealed

our friendship. On that day, the National Ministry for Children and Adolescents was born, the first national committee of the Pentecostal Church of Chile to focus on the needs of the youngest members of the church.

Pablo had joined the Chilean Army against his mother's wishes in hopes of better educational and job opportunities. Rebeca struggled with a painful clash of contradictory feelings as she sought to support her son in his decisions, while the horrible memories of the repression and human rights abuses by the military forces of Chile during the period of the dictatorship fueled her deep commitment to peace and nonviolence. Pablo, her firstborn who lit every room he entered with mischievous spunk and laughter, died early one morning with no warning, no time to brace for the loss, in a military hospital.

As I prepared to go to the wake that same day, I wandered into my bedroom absently seeking some sort of message from God to calm the ache in my heart and answer the intense pain I knew I would face as I looked through Rebeca's eyes into her brokenness. As I reached down to touch the shawl on my bed, I thought I should take it to Rebeca. I kneeled to pray, asking that if I was to give the shawl to her on God's behalf, that somehow we would have a moment alone together.

During a wake in Latin America, family members are carefully accompanied at all times. Being alone with Rebeca seemed impossible. There were people from churches throughout the country filing in and out, some in shock and others mumbling the words that seem senseless before the stark reality of death. I kept praying and waiting, holding tightly onto the strap of my backpack where I had carefully stowed the shawl. Then, it happened. I looked all around, and the people seemed to have receded into the background. Rebeca and I stepped into a sacred space where I knew we were alone, accompanied only by the divine Comforter. I wrapped the shawl around her shoulders, explaining where and how it was made. Then I explained, as we wept in each other's arms, that I hoped my prayers, along with those of the sisters who had made the shawl, might surround her with God's embrace in the pain of the coming months and years.

The next day I didn't have the chance to approach Rebeca as more friends and family members arrived for the funeral, but I could see her wearing the shawl. Her husband thanked me after the funeral, and asked if he, too, could cling to that tangible sign of God's comfort.

Last week I was at Rebeca's house for lunch. The emotional anesthetic that helps humans to survive tragedy has worn off and the pain of the loss grows more intense every day. Her questions are deeper and more difficult than what I am able to answer. I sit beside her in her growing doubt and struggle for healing. The shawl is on her bed now, and I have seen her carry it with her as she travels to the different Sunday School teacher training workshops.

From the fingers of the women in Massachusetts, through the hands and arms of a missionary, to the gentle grip around the shoulders of a mourning mother in Chile, God weaves together the lives of God's children in mysterious and wondrous ways. May we have the patience to sit alongside those near to us and far away, who need the simple comfort of our presence. We are, after all, being knit together by the clicking needles of the Savior's love and grace into a shawl large enough to embrace humanity.

JOURNAL NOTES

As I traveled throughout the United States in 2007, I told Rebeca's story in many churches. People often would come to me afterwards and share their own special prayer shawl experience with me. At University Christian Church in Fort Worth, Texas, I was given another prayer shawl. I was thrilled! A couple of weeks later, I was at a Global Ministries Board meeting in Indianapolis, and I was invited to share Rebeca's story at the morning devotions. When I finished, I stuffed my new prayer shawl into my backpack. A speaker at the meeting, whom I didn't know personally, had received news that his father had died in the Philippines and he would have to travel home immediately. I felt an urging to give him my new prayer shawl, but when he was surrounded by other people embracing him and praying for him, I decided it wasn't the Spirit's guiding, and I turned to go on to another meeting. As I walked out the door, a friend and staff member in Indianapolis came after me saying, "Elena, didn't you hear God? God said that your prayer shawl should be traveling to the Philippines!" I had ignored that quiet voice of God whispering, "This is the way, now follow it!" (Isaiah 30:21). We ran out to the hotel lobby together. I barely had time to hug and bless him, saying, "May this prayer shawl embrace you with God's love in your travels home," before he turned, visibly touched, to catch the cab to the airport. It seems that I am not supposed to keep the prayer shawls that are entrusted to me!

When I told this story in Massachusetts at a church meeting, the Reverend Karen Nell Smith wrote the following on one of the little cards that I provided in order to receive feedback and comments from the audience: "I must confess that I may be the one who knit the first prayer shawl for Elena. I remember sitting at a meeting working on it, knowing how important it was to have the knitting capture some of the essence of Elena and our shared ministries of peace. Elena comes to Massachusetts only every few years, and I knew it would be quite a while before I saw her again. I wanted her to have the prayer shawl I knit in her presence to take with her back to Chile, never imagining that it would be the beginning of a story of giving, touching the lives of others so far way, and connecting us all in a journey of peace. Now I know that this story of prayer shawls has been told many, many times. Indeed, the story continues with each new telling. Elena is an amazing storyteller. She can see God's presence in each tale and knows intuitively how to weave it into something that reflects the essence of peace-building and inspires others to reach out in peace as well. The prayer shawl story(ies) is just one example of this, as the story unfolds from one person to the next, through the hands of one group to another, from one country to other countries. It's as if the shawls themselves are simply a living metaphor for the breath of the Spirit and its healing, connecting power to transform.

"From one individual and a small congregation in Massachusetts, the power of this story has come back to us many, many times. When I first began to serve the Congregational Church of Christ (UCC) in North Leominster, Mass., as its part-time pastor, there were less than 100 active members and perhaps 30 or so in worship on a Sunday. The congregation had made the difficult decision to move from a full-time pastorate to a part-time position, a move that could be seen as failure and powerlessness by many. But instead, this small group of faithful people has become a vibrant congregation and the prayer shawl ministry and story has been part of their story of rebirth. God is using them, the work of their hands and their faithfulness in amazing, life-transforming ways. Hearing Elena's stories and knowing that they have been part of something much larger than themselves, used by God in this way, has had life-giving impact on this community of faith. Inspired over the past few years by this and other stories of prayer shawls, our ministry has grown to touch lives throughout the community of Leominster and Massachusetts, to places and people throughout the world including New Orleans and the Gulf Coast, the Pentecostal Church of Chile, Vietnam, and Beslan in the Russian Federation, and Umzinyathe in South Africa."

QUESTIONS

1. Does your church or another church you know of have a prayer shawl ministry? If so, ask the members of that ministry to share some of their stories with you.
2. Have you ever felt God whispering instructions for you to do something? Did you obey? What happened?

25

A Gathering Place

Do not be anxious about anything, but in every situation, by prayer and petition, with thanksgiving, present your requests to God.

Philippians 4:6

"What do you need to feel safe in this place?" I pose this question to every group of participants that comes to the camps, courses, or retreats at the Shalom Center when we create the community covenant at the beginning of the program. This time, I ask a group of women who have traveled into the mountains for the prayer shawl ministry retreat. It seems like a simple question, and yet many of the women weep as they dare to answer honestly, accepting the call to speak the truth in love perhaps for the first time in a group of people who they have not met before. Stitch by stitch, we begin to knit a community where we can share tears and laughter, pain and joy, frustration and success. Here we can unravel our mistakes, seek forgiveness and reconciliation, and begin to knit again.

These women have gathered from up and down Chile, and as they knit, they share and pray. One is from a rough neighborhood outside of Santiago, and she tells of raising her children as a single mother working as a live-in maid, with just enough free time on Sundays to pick her children up from her mother's house and take them to church. "My oldest son is a minister now," she states proudly. Another woman comes from the southern coast of Chile where the tsunami washed away her home along with the rest of her village. She speaks of learning to be grateful even in the midst of her loss and how knitting has helped calm her worries while keeping her hands and mind busy. Two young women are university students. They are surprised when the older women listen with respect and concern as they tell about struggling to grow in their faith under the negative pressures of friends and secular higher education. Knitting prayer shawls has become a way to keep centered, develop a prayer discipline, and to give the gift of faith to others who might have otherwise rejected it. A grandmother, daughter, and granddaughter have come together to the retreat. For them, it is a time to let go of day-to-day responsibilities, celebrate family, and reaffirm their support for each other.

Sacred space is a nexus of the right place at the precise moment. The Shalom Center is a gathering place where God invites us to step into these holy moments and places where our relationships are healed. Together we have discovered that healing can come from the simple act of wrapping a prayer shawl around the shoulders of a troubled sister, from knitting our blessings into something beautiful, or from praying and laughing together in a circle of women.

QUESTIONS

1. Does your church organize retreats for different groups? What is the value of going on a retreat?
2. How has your relationship with God, yourself, or others deepened through participating in a retreat?
3. If you could design your own retreat, who would you invite and what would you include in the program?

26

Making a Difference

Carry each other's burdens, and in this way you will
fulfill the law of Christ.

GALATIANS 6:2

Alejandra has a dream: Every day she seeks to make a difference
in someone's life even if it is in a small way.

The dream began when Alejandra was a toddler. She bumped
into a kerosene stove while playing, and within a few seconds,
had suffered burns on most of her abdomen, leg, and arm. She
spent many days throughout her early childhood in the hospital
recovering from multiple operations. So it was through personal
experience, even at a very young age, that Alejandra decided she
would find a way to help other people.

I met Alejandra when she was 17 years old. She was wearing
the typical uniform of a Chilean public high school student: dark
blue jumper and same color knee-high socks, white blouse, and
maroon tie. Her mouth was quick to laugh, but her eyes spoke of
deep compassion. Over the years, I have watched her deal with her
own trauma, choosing time and time again to accept the refining
fire of life's challenges as a source of patience, hope, joy, and peace
for her own life as well as the motivation to reach out to others.

On the morning after the February 2010 earthquake and
tsunami in Chile, Alejandra, now a nurse at the municipal clinic
of Tomé and first aid facilitator at the Shalom Center, went to
Dichato, a fishing and tourist village across the great bay from
the port of Talcahuano. Alejandra's father is the pastor of the
Pentecostal Church of Chile in the nearby town of Tomé, and he
also ministers in a mission church in Dichato. Together, she and
her father climbed over mounds of debris, carefully avoiding pits
of water left by the immense waves that flowed over the village,
and found the little mission church still standing among the piles
of cars, washing machines, beds, and refrigerators. None of the

homes of the members of the church remained.

Later that day, Alejandra finally found the sisters and brothers who belonged to the church. They were up in the hills preparing to camp, not only homeless but fearful of the constant earth tremors. One of the elderly members of the church, a widow, dressed only in a nightgown and an oversized pair of borrowed fishing boots, took Alejandra aside and asked her, head down in embarrassment, if she could please get her some underclothes.

Alejandra went right to work. First she organized the church to provide assistance in the immediate needs of dry clothing, food, clean drinking water, first aid, and shelter. Once the local government was able to catch up on these immediate needs, Alejandra began to think about how to respond to the emotional trauma of not only those from Dichato but also in the other towns and villages in the area. Alejandra had been trained in the STAR[1] program for trauma healing and resilience development at the Shalom Center, but she wanted to find a way to connect her medical training as a nurse to the spiritual and emotional wounds of the people around her. Thanks to a scholarship provided by the Shalom Center, Alejandra was able to travel to the Brookfield Institute in Massachusetts for two weeks of specialized capacity building in massage therapy and trauma healing. She returned to Tomé and Dichato to minister to many children, youth, and adults who continue to suffer the long-term effects of the disaster.

Alejandra is fulfilling her dream. She is making a difference.

QUESTIONS

1. The members of the Pentecostal Church of Chile often speak of "dreaming in the Lord," meaning to dream of doing God's will by helping build God's kingdom. Have you ever dreamt of doing something to help build God's kingdom on earth?
2. Many of the stories in this book stem from the earthquake in Chile. What life-giving stories have you heard that resulted from a natural disaster in your community or country?

---

[1]STAR: Seminars for Trauma Awareness and Resilience from the Center for Justice and Peacebuilding, Eastern Mennonite University. With the basics learned in the STAR program and the experience gained during the aftermath of the earthquake in Chile, the Shalom Center has developed the "Roots in the Ruins: Hope in Trauma" training program. During the past four years, this program has begun to train and prepare trauma healing and resilience development facilitators in churches throughout Latin American and the Caribbean thanks to the support of Global Ministries.

27

Alondra's Prayer

"Do you hear what these children are saying?" they
asked him. "Yes," replied Jesus, "have you never read,
'From the lips of children and infants you, Lord, have
called forth your praise'?"

MATTHEW 21:16

Bishop Ulises Muñoz of the Pentecostal Church of Chile had
just returned home from the hospital after a car accident when
his four-year-old granddaughter, Alondra, came to visit. He was
bruised and sore, but *"gracias a Dios"* (thanks be to God) he hadn't
suffered any major injuries. Alondra's mother explained that they
needed to be gentle with Grandpa until he recovered. Alondra
slipped into her grandparents' room and stood tall next to her
grandfather as he lay in bed. She spoke sternly and wagged her
finger, making clear her disapproval of his misbehavior: "What
game do you think you were playing? Did you do this so the police
and the firemen would come and everyone would make a fuss about
you? Listen to the phone. It is ringing with all the people who are
calling to find out if you are okay."

Next Alondra, in a very serious tone, asked her grandpa to tell
her what part of his body didn't hurt, because she was going to
pray and ask God for his healing. The bishop dutifully reached out
his hand, and Alondra bowed her head, holding his pinky finger
as she began to pray: "This little piggy went to the market!" (Of
course, it was the Spanish version, which says: "This little finger
bought an egg!")

The bus ride from Talca to Curicó normally takes about an hour,
but in the days after the February 27, 2010 earthquake with the
bridges gone and fissures crisscrossing the Pan American highway,
the trip took nearly five hours. Acsa, a young nursing student, and
I worked on an "emotional first aid" handout to share with parents
and Sunday School teachers in the communities devastated by the

earthquake and tsunami while we rode the bus. In a STAR course (Seminar in Trauma Awareness and Resilience – Eastern Mennonite University) offered by the Shalom Center in partnership with the Brookfield Institute of Massachusetts, we learned strategies to help people emotionally in the aftermath of a traumatic experience. One technique was a hand massage, whereby people could explore different feelings related to each finger. We learned that the nerve endings in each finger are connected to different parts of the brain where these feelings are processed. I remembered the story of Alondra. Little did she know that, as she held each of her grandfather's fingers, she was also helping to heal the emotional trauma of the accident.

By the time Alondra had finished her prayer with, "Wee, wee, wee all the way home," she had given her grandfather two healing gifts by praying while holding each of his fingers: one was the gift of mirth and play, and the other a memory of joy wedged into one of pain and trauma. The bishop can't help but remember Alondra's prayer each time the car accident comes to mind; a child's innate wisdom etched the path of healing with humor and physical contact.

QUESTIONS

1. Can you think of other stories where children have had words of wisdom for adults?
2. Can you think of other situations where humor has helped ease a painful memory?
3. Try a hand massage the next time you are feeling anxious or afraid!

28

Beyond the Loss

But whatever were gains to me I now consider loss for
the sake of Christ.

Philippians 3:7

I first met Hermenia Sánchez when I accompanied a delegation
from the United States on a visit to the village of San Gerardo where
she lives. The pastor of the local church, Pastor Rodrigo, asked us
if we would go to pray for Hermana Hermita, as she is known,
because she had not been feeling well.

The plants and flowers filling her front patio spilled over the
low wall and the gate, a wild array of colors and shapes glorious
in the summer sunlight. The shadowy coolness of the thick walls
of the adobe house invited us in from the heat. Hermana Hermita
sat on a rattan and wooden chair by the table waiting for us, patient
yet expectant. San Gerardo, the exuberant flower garden, and the
adobe house reminded me of people and places I knew growing
up in rural Mexico. Even the old wood-burning stove in the corner,
with a potted plant decorating the top since it was too hot for a
fire, and the curled corners of the paper wall calendar, welcomed
me and made me feel at home.

Looking back now, it is Hermana Hermita herself that stirs up
the richest memories and feelings. She greets me warmly by taking
my hand between her garlic-smelling palms and kisses me lightly
on the cheek. Her eyes dance with good humor though her legs are
painfully swollen. Her wrinkles are patterns of joy and grace even
in her old age. Her long wispy gray hair is tied back in a bun, and
her apron is worn and faded. When she speaks, I hear echoes of the
rural women in the Disciples churches of central Mexico, and I feel
like I could sit for hours at her feet basking in the wisdom of her
words. She testifies to faith and hope in the midst of life's trials. She
encourages us to seek God's kingdom in the least expected places.

She cajoles us to never give up on God because God will keep his promises. She lays her hands on our heads, including the members of the delegation, and prays for us and our families.

We have come to pray for Hermana Hermita, but it is she who has blessed us! The pastor tells us that she is not able to walk far but crosses the patio to a little chapel which she opens every day. People from all over the area, believers and non-believers, Catholic and Protestant, rich and poor, come and ask her to pray for them. She is known throughout the community as a healer.

I returned to San Gerardo with another delegation almost exactly one year later, a year of pain, heartache, and tragedy. Ever since I have lived in Chile, I have heard the elderly folk reminding the younger, "If you are in an adobe house in an earthquake, get out." Many people were saved in Chile on February 27, 2010, because they heeded these words. I remembered Hermana Hermita and her swollen legs. I knew she would be unable to move quickly, so I called San Gerardo as soon as I could after the earthquake to ask about her. Miraculously, in the midst of lost power and cell service, I got through to Pastor Rodrigo. He managed to say, "We are all okay, so is Hermana Hermita," before the call was cut off. In the whirlwind of the post-earthquake/tsunami recovery project, I was unable to return to San Gerardo for a year.

Beyond the gate and the garden, all that is left of the adobe house are the tiles from the kitchen floor. I find her sitting on a plastic chair in a makeshift house made of tin and boards salvaged from her old home. Again she welcomes me with open arms. She prays for us, thanking God that we have graced her with our visit. She tells how she and her grandchildren barely escaped from the caving walls and the crushing roof by laying down in between two beds. She asks us to bless the new prefabricated house that the municipal government has just finished for her, but she has not yet moved into. She is still full of joy and peace as she speaks of God's faithfulness. Then she breaks down and weeps when she explains that the chapel also fell in the earthquake.

Hermana Hermita lost her home and place of prayer, but she did not lose hope. The church is finishing the construction of a new chapel on the site of the old one, and soon she will be taking those few painstaking steps across the flowering patio to open the doors of the chapel. There she will listen to the needs of those in her community, and pray, now more fervently than ever, for healing beyond the loss.

QUESTIONS

1. Can you think of someone who you admire because of his or her faith?
2. What do you think is the most important characteristic of Hermana Hermita's faith?
3. How do you think a person develops a faith deep enough to carry him or her through in the time of loss?

29

Lifting Up Hope

"For I know the plans I have for you," declares the Lord,
"plans to prosper you and not to harm you, plans to give
you hope and a future."

JEREMIAH 29:11

Esperanza is a traveler. She is a toy doll made in Tomé, a seaside town in the Bío-Bío Region of southern Chile. She and 180 sister dolls have hugged hundreds of children throughout Chile in the Doors of Hope workshops for trauma healing and resilience development. One of her sisters traveled to Japan after the earthquake there.

Over the past year and a half, we have been bombarded by the heart-wrenching images in the aftermath of natural disasters: earthquakes, tornadoes, floods…And even though the images have faded from the media, the people in these countries are still struggling to rebuild their homes and their lives.

I would like for you to pretend you are a missionary in one of the countries or areas where there has been a natural disaster. Imagine that you have been in this country for quite a few years, and that you have worked in partnership with a national church. What would you do to lift up hope in children, youth, and adults who were affected? What would you do right away? What would you plan for in a year or five years? How would you spend your time, energy, and limited resources in the short and long run?

I never thought I would be developing an emergency aid program, and if someone had asked me at the time of the earthquake if I was ready for what was coming, I would have said that nothing had prepared me to be in Chile under those circumstances. Looking back now, however, I can see many ways in which God equipped me to be in the right place at the right time. Because of the work at the Shalom Center, I knew builders, architects, nurses, pastors, and community leaders; I had simple but essential resources like tents, flashlights, blankets, clothes, water jugs, and first aid kits; I had training in emergency preparedness, first aid, conflict transformation, trauma healing, and resilience development; I had a team of willing, dedicated, and responsible Shalom Center and Sunday School volunteers scattered in local communities throughout the disaster zone.

"What can I do?" was the question everyone asked. I think the most important role I played was to help channel the energy and skills of the hundreds of people who wanted to help. Some helped to clean up while others built Blessing Cabins. Some raised funds and offerings while others collected and delivered nonperishable food items throughout the long winter months. Still others were trained in emotional first aid and tended to traumatized children, youth, and adults.

Many of the women from the Pentecostal Church of Chile in the Tomé area lost everything either in the earthquake or the tsunami, but they, too, wanted to do something for others. They gathered for weeks to cut, sew, and bless the Esperanza dolls that would be given to each of the workshop leaders sent to the local communities to work with children in the Doors of Hope program: the trauma healing and resilience development component of the "Lift Up Hope" recovery project. "While making these dolls," one of the women said to me, "I wept for everything I lost. But, as I worked with my sisters from the church, I knew I was not alone. As each doll was finished, I could feel my faith strengthen. I prayed for each child that would hug Esperanza, and I, too, embraced hope."

QUESTIONS

1. "Esperanza" means hope. What gives you hope in the midst of difficult situations?
2. What would you do with your gifts and abilities to help others in the midst of a natural disaster?
3. As young people, we oftentimes dream of doing great things for others. Why is being faithful in the small and seemingly insignificant things just as important?

30

If You Pray, You Will Know You Are Not Alone

Rejoice in the Lord always. I will say it again: Rejoice!
Let your gentleness be evident to all. The Lord is near.
Do not be anxious about anything, but in every situation,
by prayer and petition, with thanksgiving, present
your requests to God. And the peace of God, which
transcends all understanding, will guard your hearts
and your minds in Christ Jesus.

PHILIPPIANS 4:4-7

"My name is Saray. I am eight years old and in the third grade. I live with my mother, father, and baby brother on the coast of Chile. My favorite time of the year is Christmas, when all of my cousins come to visit. I feel good when I play with my friends or when I am having fun with my family. I like to go to church, especially Sunday School. I hope to help other people when I grow up."

I called Saray's mother on the phone a couple of weeks before I was to visit, asking if I could interview her spunky red-haired daughter. Saray answered my questions with earnest seriousness. I have known Saray since she was a baby, and we have often played together, but the thought of an interview with the corresponding photo session made her feel excited and grown up.

I wanted to interview Saray to learn more about children and their resilience. I had recently read an article in a leading Chilean newspaper that quoted statistics for the 2010 school year after 1,000 earthquake-damaged school buildings in Chile had to be abandoned. The article stated that there had been a shocking increase in bullying in elementary and high schools throughout the country during this one school year. However, neither this article nor any other I read associated the alarming increase in school violence with the trauma of the national disaster. I invited Saray to think back on this year and tell me what had been helpful and what had made her more resilient.

"I was awake when the earthquake started because I had gone to the bathroom," she said. "My mom and dad jumped out of bed and took me to the kitchen because it was safer there. I was very afraid. Our house moved but it didn't fall down. We went to my grandparents' house as soon as the earth stopped shaking because they live up the hill from the beach. Our house had to be fixed as a result of the earthquake, so I stayed with my grandparents a long time. After the earthquake I had nightmares and. . . ." Saray pauses and says with a hint of embarrassment, "Are you going to tell other people everything I say?" "I will only share what you give me permission to share," I promise her. "Well," she continues, "I guess it is okay for you to tell people since I will probably never meet them anyway." She pauses again and whispers, "I started wetting my bed. I am too big to be afraid to go to the bathroom at night. What was really embarrassing was that I was staying at my grandparents' house, and sometimes I would come into a room and the adults would suddenly change the subject. I knew they were talking about me. The person who was most helpful was my aunt. She really listened to me. We both decided that maybe it would be good for me to talk to a psychologist at the same clinic where she works. The psychologist told me to imagine a warm, red blanket protecting me whenever I am afraid. But I didn't do exactly what she told me; I did something better! I started imagining when I go to bed at night that it is God who is tucking me in and covering me with a blanket. It is my special time now when I pray and feel God close so I am not afraid."

Saray's grandfather is the pastor of a local congregation of the Pentecostal Church of Chile in the heart of the disaster zone. Within a couple of days, supplies came pouring into the church to help the victims of the tsunami and the earthquake. Clothing, food, cleaning utensils, and household wares had to be sorted and packaged according to the necessities of the affected families. Saray gave herself the responsibility of gleaning baby clothing from the boxes and checking the lists to send what would be needed by each family to keep the littlest girls and boys warm, clean, and healthy. She worked for several months while waiting for school to start. Like her house, her school was not safe and also had to have major repairs. Her school eventually reconvened in the building of another local church. "I wanted to go back to school, but since I couldn't, it helped me feel strong and happy to know that I was helping other people, especially the babies, even when I was very frightened myself."

"My best friend at school is Antonia. She has diabetes, but we always take care of each other. This year at school, something sad and bad happened to me. Another girl made me be friends with her and told me I had to stop being friends with Antonia. She told me she would hit me and tell lies about me if tried to be friends with anyone but her. When the teacher made us share the same desk, I couldn't concentrate because I was afraid of her. I started getting bad grades. One day, my mother found a nasty note I had written about Antonia. She asked me about it, and I started to cry. I told my mother that this other girl had made me write it. I wanted to know why this girl was so mean to Antonia and me. My mother explained that this girl's parents were getting a divorce, and that they had had many problems this year. They had lost their home in the earthquake. My mother talked to the teacher and together they promised to help me, Antonia, and the other girl."

Few people who know Saray, with all her joy and energy, know that she was born with an extremely rare skin tumor; she is the only person in Chile with this disease. There are only five other cases in the world and no known cure. This year, she had to stay in bed for two weeks because of an infection related to the cancer. Knowing that it would be a very difficult experience for this lively child to have to stay in bed during her summer vacation, I sent her a tub of pony beads and elastic string. Saray spent the time in bed making "resilience bracelets." When I visited her, she said, "I have prayed for each one of these bracelets. Now I want you to take them with you to the United States and give them to people to say 'thank you' for all the ways they helped us after the earthquake. Give them also to children who need them."

"I guess having the tumor has made me more aware of other people who are hurting," Saray said. Because she has a loving family, caring teachers, good friends, opportunities to help others, and a growing faith, Saray continues to develop resilience in the midst of life's challenges.

At the end of the interview, I asked Saray if she had the opportunity to encourage children in the United States, what she would like to say to them. She answered, "Tell the children who were in the tornadoes and floods that God is always with them and won't ever leave them. Tell the children who have cancer that when they pray, they will know that God is always beside them. Tell people that if they pray, they'll know they are not alone."

JOURNAL NOTES

Saray's story was a favorite the last time I visited churches in the United States, and many people have written to ask how she is doing. Saray is now thirteen, and in spite of being a normal teenager with the mood swings and the new fascination with boys, she still has a compassionate concern for people in need. The tumor on her leg has slowly reduced in size while the specialists debate whether to operate or to wait and see what happens when she finishes growing. Saray told me recently that the tumor is a tiny part of her life but it is not her whole life. She will not let the tumor determine who she is or what she dreams of becoming. She wants you to remember her as the girl who helped others in the earthquake even when she was very afraid herself, not as the girl who had the rare form of incurable cancer.

QUESTIONS

1. Resilience is the capacity to stand back up when a problem has knocked you down, or the ability to keep going even in the face of extreme difficulties. What makes you resilient?
2. How can life's challenges, even very difficult ones like facing an earthquake or an illness, make us more resilient?
3. Have you ever heard the term "post-traumatic growth"? What do you think it means in light of Saray's story?

31

Church at Its Best

...so in Christ we, though many, form one body, and
each member belongs to all the others.

ROMANS 12:5

I sat down on the curb next to him. I think he may have been
in the first or second grade, his glazed eyes staring out from a dirty
mask-like face. Only three days had passed since February 27 when
one of the largest earthquakes in recorded history destroyed this
boy's rural home along with thousands of other buildings. He
didn't answer when I asked him his name, but he held tightly to a
yellow checkered bag that a Sunday School teacher had just given
to him. I suggested that we look inside the bag together, and when
he didn't respond, I gently opened it for him.

First I pulled out a pencil and asked the boy, "What is this?"
His eyes were vacant, and he could not answer me. "Pencil,"
I said kindly and, after a pause, I handed it to him. I took up a
toothbrush. I asked the boy, "What is this?" His blank eyes tried to
focus. "Toothbrush," I said, and he softly repeated, "toothbrush,"
a small glimmer of recognition flitting across his face. Then I held
up a comb, and before I could speak, he stammered, "c-c-c-omb,
comb." "Yes!" I exclaimed, "it is a comb!" Little by little we worked
our way through the bag, and by the time we finished identifying
all of the objects, he was smiling and speaking with confidence.

The health and school kits shared with the children in Chile
after the disaster are an example of Church at its best. The school
supplies were collected by congregations of the Pentecostal Church
of Chile, while the health kits traveled with art supplies in suitcases
that came from churches all over the United States. We are the
Church and our gifts, from the south and the north, so different
and yet essential, are lovingly stuffed into bright-colored bags
and sent out to bless people around the world. We are the body

of Christ sitting patiently on the curb and bringing hope to a little boy with sparkling eyes.

QUESTIONS

1. When have you been really proud of being a part of the Church?
2. Have you ever helped make school kits or health kits? Where were the kits sent? What did you learn about that place or country in preparing the kits?
3. What do you think we receive as part of the body of Christ stretched around the world?

Lessons
from
Nature

The "Tres Cuernos" (Three Horns)
Mountain at the Shalom Center in the
fall of 2014.

32

Arelis Painted the Moon

The heavens declare the glory of God; the skies proclaim
the work of his hands.

Psalm 19:1

There was a full moon that cloudless night. The silvery light
cascaded down from the heavens, casting a glow over the cracks
that opened up in the ground, the boulders that broke loose from
the mountains, and the water that rose up from the ocean, hurling
itself against the shore. The moonlight did not quiver when the
earth shook.

The children remember the moon. They camped out in its light
either because their homes were gone or because their parents were
wary of moving back inside in the midst of the constant aftershocks.

"We didn't have electricity, but it was okay because the moon
was very bright."

"My grandfather told us stories every night, and it was better
than watching television."

"Whenever I see the full moon, now, I remember the
earthquake."

Environmental education and the care of God's creation have
always been at the core of my ministry as a missionary. In Chile,
after the devastation caused by the natural forces of the earthquake
and tsunami, many children and adults lost their confidence in
the stability and security of the earth and needed to restore their
relationship with the planet itself. I hoped that the beauty and
tranquility of nature could also be a source of healing.

Nine full moons after the natural disaster, more than a hundred
children from the "Creacción[1]" environmental education clubs

---

[1]"Creacción" is the environmental education program for elementary school
age children at the Shalom Center. It is a word play joining the words for creation
and action in Spanish.

formed by the Shalom Center in schools and churches gathered for a day of "re-creation" to renew their relationship with the earth. The children chose to participate in several different play-workshops including, "Water, the Source of Life," "Dirt Made My Lunch," and "My Garbage Can Talk." At noon, each group prepared an exhibit of what they had learned during the past months in their separate clubs. The children from the village of Tutuquén Bajo captured their impressions and feelings about the environment in paintings. The boards and the frames for the paintings were salvaged from materials either discarded from destroyed buildings or left over from the reconstruction. All of the children in Tutuquén Bajo lived outside after the earthquake when their adobe homes became uninhabitable, and watched the moon wane as the days turned into weeks.

Arelis painted the moon shining down on the snowcapped Andes Mountains. In her painting, the night is not frightening. It is a place where animals sleep in warm safe burrows, flowers bloom, and mushrooms suddenly sprout. The trunk of a chopped tree biodegrades and enriches the green soil with new life. A new branch sprouts from the old trunk. Across the painting, Arelis wrote one of my favorite quotes, attributed by Helen Keller to her teacher, Anne Sullivan, in her book *The Story of My Life*: "The best and most beautiful things in the world cannot be seen or even touched, but just felt in the heart." The painting is one of my cherished treasures, a reminder to me that the relationship with the earth is also part of our search for wholeness.

QUESTIONS

1. Have you ever had an experience where you felt that nature helped you heal?
2. How can having a close relationship with nature help us to develop resilience?

33

Whale Tale

You will go out in joy and be led forth in peace; the mountains and hills will burst into song before you, and all the trees of the field will clap their hands.

Isaiah 55:12

It had been a particularly difficult year in my ministry in Chile. There had been disappointments and struggles, terrifying conflicts with an antagonist looming in the shadows, too much work and not enough play. Slowly my sense of joy and zest for life dissipated like the last wisp of smoke at the end of a cheerful fire. During a visit to the United States, a wise friend, a woman minister, recognized my urgent need to take a step back and gain some perspective. She invited me on a boat ride around Cape Cod off Plymouth, Massachusetts.

As we leaned over the railing of the boat, watching the wake churn up the water, she listened while I complained. "I don't know if I am getting anywhere in Chile. Why hasn't God intervened to show me the way? I wonder if God cares. Sometimes I even wonder if God exists." No sooner had the words fallen out of my mouth when a whale breached scarcely a few yards from the side of the boat and flipped back into the water, gently spraying us. Within minutes, we spotted five or six whale tails flagging the horizon, a school of dolphins dancing around the prow of the boat, and another whale feeding with her calf in slow bubbly circles. The guide onboard kept saying over and over, "Wow! I have never seen anything like this before!" We were speechless.

My friend finally broke the silence after it looked like God's creation show had come to an end. All she said was, "Do you have any other questions?!"

JOURNAL NOTES

I told this story to a group of high school students at Camp Christian in Ohio one evening during vespers. A couple of days later, eight of these kids rushed up to me so excited they could hardly keep from all talking at once. They told me that they had been walking through camp discussing God's whale tail answer to my doubts and questions. One stated, "God has never spoken to me that way." The others agreed while someone said, "I wish God would be present in my doubts in some tangible way." No sooner had they nodded in agreement when a red fox jumped out on the path in front of them, paused with a penetrating look at the group, and ran off down the path. None of the youths had ever seen a wild fox before. They were ecstatic and full of awe as the Lord of Creation heard their doubts and answered with the gift of a fox tale of their own to share and savor.

QUESTIONS

1. Where do you look for answers when you doubt God?
2. Have you ever felt that God gave you an answer through nature?

34

In for the Long Haul

Do not withhold your mercy from me, Lord; may your
love and faithfulness always protect me.

PSALM 40:11

It was late at night when we packed up all of our camping
equipment and headed out to the Shalom Center property in central
Chile. At about one in the morning, we passed by the shack of the
lumberman who cuts firewood and makes charcoal. One of his
big dogs, an old, gray- and yellow-striped fellow, followed behind
us, two women alone in a pickup truck. He wagged his tail as we
unloaded our equipment into the little trailer house, and made
himself a bed just outside the door, establishing himself as our
official guard dog for the length of our stay. We began to wonder
if this dog might have been one of those bumbling guardian angels
who are made fun of in the movies.

The next morning, when we walked to the waterfall, he went
with us. I kept insisting that we shouldn't feed him anything or else
he would never leave and would hang around the Shalom Center
when the participants arrived. We decided to climb down the steep
path that goes to the pool at the base of the waterfall, and the dog
happily joined us on the adventure. As we were hopping from
boulder to boulder down the streambed to the pool, the dog jumped
along behind us. Suddenly, he slipped on the smooth surface of
a rock and fell whining and yelping into the ice cold stream. He
landed in a painful heap and paddled shivering and shaking to a
shallower part surrounded by deeper pools. In the middle of this
mishap, Our Dog got his name. From then on, we were forced to
pay attention to Our Dog and take better care of him. After some
encouragement and a few pushes, Our Dog finally was able to get
out of the pool and shake himself off, apparently none the worse
for the dunking. We thought for sure he had had enough and

would abandon us, heading back to a less dangerous life at the lumberman's house. Little did we know we should have named Our Dog "Old Faithful." When we left him at the base of a boulder and climbed up to get a full view of the pool with the waterfall plunging toward us over the edge of the cliff above, he whined and cried until we finally gave him a knee up and bolstered his courage with the temptation of a saltine cracker. He waited around patiently while we looked for rocks, took pictures, and painted.

On the way back along the streambed, we were careful to choose a path Our Dog could follow, but when we climbed down a fallen tree trunk, with another misstep of his rather deformed claws and feet, his body slipped halfway in a six-foot hole. Beverly, who was behind me, managed to grab him so he wouldn't go crashing all the way down, and I scrambled back up the fallen log in time to pull his tail out. He hugged Beverly's leg with all four paws and tucked his head under her arm, trembling. After enticing him with more saltines, we managed to convince him to let go and climb across another rock. I wondered if all guardian angels were as sweet, kind, and uncoordinated. He earned his way into our hearts, and we were, of course, obligated to start feeding him.

After the hike to the bottom of the waterfall, we headed down the path toward the river, and he wagged his tail in relief when we turned toward the top of the cliff and chose the overlook instead of heading down to the rocks. He followed us to the latrine and when we went stargazing on the big rock lookout. We kept him from tripping near the edge, since we were pretty sure we wouldn't be able to rescue him from the fifty-foot drop to the river below. He kept the stray cows and bulls away from the campsite and tried his hardest to snap away the bees that swarmed near us when we ate. He waited patiently whenever we stopped to take pictures or contemplate the beauty of the Andes Mountains.

When we decided to go up to the national forest to watch the sunset, we had a problem. Our Dog would not be welcome in the reserve. He didn't complain at all when we tied him up at the camp and left him a big plate of food. We came back after dark and he was lying calmly outside the door of the trailer, waiting patiently, trusting that we would come back to untie him. On the final morning before breaking camp and returning to the city, we sat on the rock in front of the waterfall with the sun on our backs and Our Dog at our feet, and we read from the daily lectionary:

¹ I waited patiently for the Lord;
    he turned to me and heard my cry.
² He lifted me out of the slimy pit,
    out of the mud and mire;
he set my feet on a rock
    and gave me a firm place to stand.
³ He put a new song in my mouth,
    a hymn of praise to our God.
Many will see and fear the Lord
    and put their trust in him.
⁴ Blessed is the one
    who trusts in the Lord,
who does not look to the proud,
    to those who turn aside to false gods.
⁵ Many Lord my God,
    are the wonders you have done,
    the things you planned for us.
None can compare with you;
    were I to speak and tell of your deeds,
    they would be too many to declare.
⁶ Sacrifice and offering you did not desire—
    but my ears you have opened—
    burnt offerings and sin offerings you did not require.
⁷ Then I said, "Here I am, I have come—
    it is written about me in the scroll
⁸ I desire to do your will, my God;
    your law is within my heart."
⁹ I proclaim your saving acts in the great assembly;
    I do not seal my lips, Lord,
    as you know.
¹⁰ I do not hide your righteousness in my heart;
    I speak of your faithfulness and your saving help.
I do not conceal your love and your faithfulness
    from the great assembly.
¹¹ Do not withhold your mercy from me, Lord;
    may your love and faithfulness always protect me.

PSALM 40:1-11

Our Dog was God's way of teaching us a valuable lesson about faithfulness. Faithfulness doesn't require a high IQ or great athletic abilities. Faithfulness is a stick-to-it-ness that leads us through dangerous paths, to cliff edges under starlit skies, on cow chases, and to patient waits just outside the latrine. Faithfulness over the long haul is an essential element to usher in the kingdom of shalom.

QUESTIONS

1. Have you had a special relationship with a pet?
2. In the story, the dog is an example of faithfulness. What other values and lessons might we learn from animals?

35

Dreams Blessed

Trust in the Lord and do good; dwell in the land and
enjoy safe pasture. Take delight in the Lord, and he will
give you the desires of your heart.

PSALM 37:3-4

I was curled up in my sleeping bag midmorning before the final
worship service on the last day of camp. Yes, I was hiding, and no,
I wasn't sleeping. The theme for the summer camps at the Shalom
Center, chosen by the staff, was "Dreaming with Shalom" and the
guiding image, *metamorphosis*. We meditated on the processes that
God uses in challenging us to grow as we reach for our dreams.

Though the sounds were a little muffled through the weight of
the sleeping bag, I could hear the participants and staff walk to the
porch of the Welcome House as the worship service began. "God
invites us to submit to the process of transformation. It may be
painful and confusing at times, but we can trust that our lives will
unfold with the beauty of butterfly wings." With a guitar playing
softly in the background, I began to move slowly at first. Then as
the music rose in crescendo, so did my struggle to get out of my
chrysalis sleeping bag. Finally, with a dramatic push, I slipped
out of the sleeping bag and stood, raising my arms as if they were
wings drying in the sun. At the very same instant that I raised my
arms, a real butterfly, a rare one far away from the rocky outcrops
where they are usually found, came fluttering into the circle. It
landed delicately first on one participant and then another. No
words were necessary.

We knew God had sent an invitation, stamped on butterfly
wings, to keep dreaming.

Keyla, a twenty-year-old college student, shared with me
later: "When I arrived at the Shalom Center, I had many doubts
and questions. My heart desired an answer from God; I wanted to
feel forgiveness for something I had done. On the hike yesterday,

when we stopped at the waterfall, I began to weep, realizing how small I am before God's greatness. I prayed, asking for a sign, but it didn't come until today. When the butterfly touched me softly, in the closing worship, I knew God was blessing the dream that was in my heart. I felt forgiveness. God has become real to me again."

QUESTIONS

1. Butterflies are often used as a metaphor for spiritual life. Why? What other images from nature could help explain our spiritual pilgrimage?
2. Have you or anyone you know ever experienced a spiritual "metamorphosis"? What changed?

36

Putting It into Practice

Because of the tender mercy of our God, by which the
rising sun will come to us from heaven to shine on those
living in darkness and in the shadow of death, to guide
our feet into the path of peace.

LUKE 1:78-79

"I have lived in shalom!" Milca was bubbling with excitement
when we met at the Shalom Center after she had spent two weeks
volunteering with the Chilean National Forest Service. Milca is a
vivacious and talented college student and a committed member of
the Pentecostal Church of Chile. It has been my honor to accompany
her in her spiritual walk from the time she was fourteen and began
attending camp at the Shalom Center.

   "When I went in to the interview for this volunteer position,
I saw that the other young people were from wealthy families
and had all the latest outdoor gear." Milca's parents are pastors
of the Pentecostal Church of Chile in the tiny village of Las
Cabras (literally "The Goats") in central Chile. While her family
struggles to pay for Milca and her sister to attend college, both
girls study and work part-time in a grocery store. "But as I started
to answer the interviewer's questions, I relaxed. He asked me
basic questions about the biodiversity of Chile, about ways of
caring for the environment such as leaving no trace and garbage
control, about camping, and about teamwork. He asked me what
I would do if I knew that one of the other volunteers was drinking
even after signing a "no drinking, no smoking, no drugs" policy
commitment—if I would try to talk to the volunteer or if I would
talk to a supervisor. I answered that I would talk to the supervisor
immediately, because I felt it would do no good to talk to the
volunteer myself if a commitment had already been broken, that
the drinking could put us all in danger, and that I felt that caring
for ourselves, our bodies, and our relationships was directly tied to

caring for the environment. The interviewer told me that in all of his years of interviewing young people for this volunteer service, he had never heard the answers I had given him. I spent the next hour sharing with him the vision and mission of the Shalom Center, and I what I have learned as a volunteer on staff at this church camp of the Pentecostal Church of Chile."

Milca continued. "When I arrived at the national forest located on the 'Todos los Santos'[1] Lake in southern Chile, I felt like a very tiny and insignificant fish in a large and strange pond. Everything was different from how we do things at the Shalom Center. I was intimidated by the rough language, gossip, and trivial infighting between leaders and volunteers. I prayed. I felt the Holy Spirit guide me. I visited the volunteers in each of the tents every night with questions to help them think deeply about their experiences during the day. This is one of the responsibilities of the motivators[2] at the Shalom Center. Soon the leaders were asking me to lead group development activities. Then I began making suggestions with regard to the program.

"On the second-to-last day of work, we were hauling construction materials about five miles up a mountain to repair a scenic overlook on a trail when it began to rain. Our team leader suggested that we climb three miles further to the nearest refuge. I felt God speak to me in my heart with an urgency I could not ignore. I insisted that we needed to get back to the base camp immediately. Since I had already made a name for myself by listening to others, working hard, and encouraging the leaders, he followed my advice. By the time we had crossed the swollen rivers and climbed down the muddy paths, we discovered that the base camp had been evacuated due to flash flood warnings. During the next weeks, no one was able to traverse that trail because it was too dangerous. If we had stayed, we would have been stuck on the mountain. Once we caught up with the rest of the volunteers at the nearest hostel, the group leader thanked me in front of the whole camp.

"The national leader of the volunteer service asked me to be a part of the staff next year. I told him that I had other obligations with my church, and that I felt that I still needed further training at the Shalom Center before taking on such a responsibility. As I got off the bus on the highway outside of 'Las Cabras,' the other

---

[1] All Saints Lake

[2] At the Shalom Center, counselors are called "motivators" while those on the teaching staff are called "facilitators."

volunteers hung out the windows shouting and cheering. Back when I was picked from hundreds of young people to volunteer in the Chilean National Forest Service, my parents thought it would be a perfect opportunity for me to preach God's word. It was, but not in any way they could have imagined. I preached, with my actions, about God's invitation to SHALOM as I have learned at the Shalom Center. I practiced, in the midst of those who don't know God, the Bible text that is the theme of the Shalom Center:

> because of the tender mercy of our God,
>> by which the rising sun will come to us from heaven
> to shine on those living in darkness
>> and in the shadow of death,
> to guide our feet into the path of peace. (Luke 1:78-79)

"For two weeks, I showed the people of the National Forest Service what I have learned at my church camp: that to truly care for the environment, we must work on healing our relationships—with God, with ourselves, with others, and with all of creation."

QUESTIONS

1. Have you, or someone you know, had the opportunity to go to church camp or some other camp program? What was memorable about the experience?
2. In what ways was Milca able to preach with actions louder than words? Can you remember an occasion where you were able to put your faith into practice as Milca did?
3. What do you think about the last phrase from the story: "to truly care for the environment, we must work on healing our relationships—with God, with ourselves, with others, and with all of creation?"

37

Diversity

I know that you can do all things; no purpose of yours can be thwarted. You asked, "Who is this that obscures my plans without knowledge?" Surely I spoke of things I did not understand, things too wonderful for me to know. You said, "Listen now, and I will speak; I will question you, and you shall answer me." My ears had heard of you but now my eyes have seen you. Therefore I despise myself and repent in dust and ashes.

JOB 42:2-6

My mother always says she is glad that she hears about my adventures as a missionary after I am home safe and sound. One of those memorable adventures took place when I joined two other young women on a long bus ride to the Pantanal, the largest swamp in the world. Our adventures in southern Brazil remain in my memory as unforgettable lessons in nature's classroom. It was through those experiences that I learned the basic, intrinsic value of diversity in nature and among people as an expression of God's creativity and imagination. Diversity, exposed in millions of different plants, insects, animals, and people, is a mystery that stretches the limits of our understanding and a fingerprint that gives evidence to the unfathomable magnitude of the Creator.

Diversity demands that we develop a profound respect for life in all of its different manifestations. To this day, I am not really sure how we ended up riding with eight other women from six different countries in a dilapidated pickup truck that broke down multiple times on an abandoned dirt road going into the swamp. It took all day, but we finally arrived at a campsite set up by our Brazilian and Danish guides at the edge of one of the tributaries of the Paraguay River. We laughed over dinner, trying to understand the mix of English, Spanish, Portuguese, German, Danish, and French. Then, exhausted from the journey, we decided to get ready for bed. One of my friends and I headed down to the edge of the water to brush our teeth. Suddenly, I spotted two green marbles in the water about four feet from where we were standing. With my mouth foaming with toothpaste, I asked my friend what she thought those pale lights were. When she turned on her flashlight, we discovered that the marbles were the eyes of a nine-foot alligator. We almost choked on our toothpaste as we carefully stepped backward, away from the water's edge. The next morning, the guide showed us the carcass of another alligator near where we had been standing. He explained that the dead alligator had been the companion to the one we had seen in the water, but while they had been away from camp a few weeks before, poachers had killed it. Suddenly our fear of the solitary alligator turned into a new appreciation for life so easily snatched away.

Diversity invites us into a new awareness of the world we inhabit and into a sense of awe before the Creator's magnificent handiwork. One afternoon in the Pantanal, the Brazilian guide offered to take us on a long hike through an area of grasslands. Just as the sun was touching the tips of the tall grasses and painting them yellow, red, and orange, our guide motioned us to be quiet and to follow him quickly. As he headed off the trail, I thought of snakes, but he trotted confidently toward a large, shaggy, dark figure. When we were just a few yards away, I recognized the animal: it was a giant anteater. The guide told us it was one of the largest he had ever seen, measuring well over six feet from its long snout to the tip of its stringy tail. The whole scene still fills me with wonder as I remember the sun sinking slowly down into the horizon, the anteater snuffing the ground looking for dinner, the howler monkeys screaming in the distance, the dozens of different bird calls, and the burnt sweet smell of the toasted grass.

Appreciating diversity requires humility and patience. Our Danish guide told us that it wasn't the anacondas, alligators, poisonous snakes, or jaguars that bothered him about living in the middle of the swamp. It was the insects. The insects showed no prejudice; they were completely impartial. They stung and bit us all: Europeans, North Americans, South Americans, rich, poor, thin, fat, short, tall, pretty, ugly. To the insects we were all the same, and no one could take on airs of superiority. No one could claim to be free of the itching. It is amazing how humbling a good itch can be. The constant buzzing, whining, flying, crawling in our hair, under our clothes, and even inside our shoes while we were wearing them sorely tried our patience. There were two choices: to go mad or to accept the fact that the insects ruled the Pantanal.

Opening ourselves to exploring the diversity of life is a risky business. Our participation in the discovery process can radically change our perspectives and beliefs about ourselves, about others, and about God. We went fishing in the Pantanal. We were as excited as school boys playing hooky as we made some old-fashioned cane poles, grabbed a container of chicken innards, and set out single-file along the path beside the river, crossing the waist deep water several times. As we found a quiet corner, the guide said, "This is a good place to fish." In a few minutes, I felt the first bite. When the fish landed on the bank squirming and flapping, I recognized its large, razor sharp, white teeth. Piranhas! I stuck a stick as thick as my thumb in its mouth, and with one snap of the powerful jaws, it split in two. The guide calmly told us that where there are still waters, there are piranhas, and where there are piranhas, there are alligators. Suddenly the happy and rollicking hike along the river turned frightening and ominous. In our ignorance, we had followed our guide wading from bank to bank. We would have to retrace our steps now knowing that we would be sharing the river with piranhas and alligators. Whereas before we had been oblivious to the danger and the need to trust our guide, now we paid close attention to his indications and carefully followed his lead.

Nothing had changed in the environment from the time we started on the hike to when we got back to camp and broiled our large catch of fish, yet everything seemed different. We had been transformed. Through our new knowledge, we were forced to accept the swamp as a full package, with all of its beauty stretching out before us and with its dangers lurking in the calm waters. Perhaps this fine line between fear and curiosity—the unknown and the yet to be discovered, the safe and the dangerous, the tension we experience as we explore the earth's diversity—is the same as when we enter into new relationships with others or dare to open our lives to God.

QUESTIONS

1. This story proposes the idea that nature's diversity is God's fingerprint. How might this same principle apply to people?
2. What other characteristics of God might be revealed through nature?
3. What is the most important lesson you have learned from nature?

38

Dead Horse

How many are your works, Lord! In wisdom you made
them all; the earth is full of your creatures.

PSALM 104:24

Delicate strands of dew, like a jeweled net, sparkle before
me as I walk down the path of the forest at the Shalom Center in
central Chile. A spider has been working all night, spinning and
sending strands that connect a leaf here, a branch there, and a twig
somewhere just out of sight overhead. The web spans the path,
and I choose to sit in the morning sun meditating on this natural
tapestry rather than tear my way through the sticky masterpiece.
It is the web that begins to weave together experiences, thoughts,
and questions in my mind. I have always known, intuitively, that
everything and everyone was connected in an intricate pattern, but
in the past few years, as I have begun my personal and professional
search for shalom, the mysteries of the web of life have glistened
in a new light.

Like the spider spinning a beautiful and complex weaving,
the entire universe is connected through invisible threads of
interdependence. I can imagine the Creator at the beginning of
time delighting in balancing and counterbalancing galaxies, suns,
planets, gases, minerals, microbes, plants, and animals. Every part
of creation was formed in perfect synchrony with every other part—
each unique and whole, and yet an essential piece of something
greater. Nature, with its spectacular sunsets, cascading waterfalls,
rhythmic ocean waves, and newborn butterflies, is the evidence of
God's unfolding dream of shalom for all that was created.

Nature teaches us to look for the evidence of God's handiwork
in the least likely places. I look more closely at the spider web
across the path. The shell of a dead fly caught in the sticky strands
of the web and sucked dry by the spider reminds me of a strange
encounter with *shalom*.

When we were searching through the foothills of the Andes Mountains for the property where the Shalom Center would be established, my brother and I visited a piece of land on the Duqueco River in south-central Chile. As we approached the sloping hills covered with trees, my heart began to race with excitement. I caught sight of the snowcapped volcanoes in the distance and the river gently winding its way through a valley patched by trees and open spaces. Could this be the perfect place for a camp, retreat center, and nature reserve?

The first thing we smelled, just inside the property gate, was a dead horse. Even from a distance, its rotting stench and disgusting appearance marred the awe-inspiring scenery. But as we walked past the carcass, I experienced an extraordinary shift in perspective. Suddenly, I noticed that the forests on this land and on all the surrounding hillsides were not forests at all but pine tree plantations, exotic imports to Chile for timber production. The soil, as often happens under the stress of constant planting and clear cutting, was severely eroded. The acid from the pine needles had changed the composition of the soil and there were few bushes, plants, or flowers making up the undergrowth. The enormous patches of open areas were actually spaces denuded of all vegetation with leftover trunks and branches piled high ready to be burned. The water in the river was muddied by the erosion of the soil, and there were dead fish and piles of garbage along its shores. It was the silence, however, that stopped me in my tracks and made me turn slowly around. I could not hear any birds sing nor insects hum. Only the wind wept softly in the pine branches. The hills that seemed so pristine and splendid from a distance, up close became a virtual wasteland.

And the dead horse...I looked at it up close as I walked by, pinching my nose. The maggots and bugs were doing their work, and I could see some kind of bird, perhaps and Andean Condor but more likely a vulture, circling far overhead. Soon the carrion would completely decompose and become part of the nutrients in the soil to give new life. Nothing would be wasted, and nature would complete its efficient and enriching clean-up work. What seemed from afar to be a picture-perfect image turned out to be the tragic forces of destruction at work. What seemed at first to be the putrid smell of decay actually was the power of life, hope, and restoration in action. What may seem to be *shalom* turns out to be injustice masquerading as peace or untruth deceiving in the name of mercy. What may seem to be the desperate and irreparable stench of death may actually be the healthy process of transformation giving birth to reconciliation, hope, harmony, and well being.

The sun has almost dried the dew on the spider web, and the spider appears to repair a strand that has unraveled during the night. I decide it is time to continue on my hike, but not without first thanking the spider for the pause along the path and the opportunity for musings and reflections. I am beginning to understand how *shalom* is God's delicate web of creation spun anew with exquisite and surprising threads, even in the midst of the brokenness caused by careless humans bumbling along the path.

QUESTIONS

1. In the story, a dead horse is compared to God's work of resurrection and reconciliation. Do you have your own experience of discovering God in an unexpected situation?
2. The Hebrew word "shalom" appears often in this book. After reading the book, how would you define "shalom"?
3. What do you think are the most important values we must uphold if we are to help build God's kingdom of shalom?
4. How are healing and the development of resilience essential to that shalom kingdom?

CPSIA information can be obtained
at www.ICGtesting.com
Printed in the USA
LVOW10s1538200617

538737LV00004B/582/P